THE SOLUTION

THE SOLUTION

A Revolutionary Plan to Eliminate School Shootings, Child Suicide, and the Silent Mental Turmoil Destroying Our Kids

Written by Sarah Amedeo

Published by Quantum Roots Publishing Oswego, IL

Printed in the United States of America.

ISBN: 979-8-9949627-0-1

Library of Congress Control Number: 2026901618

Cover Design: Neslihan Yardimli

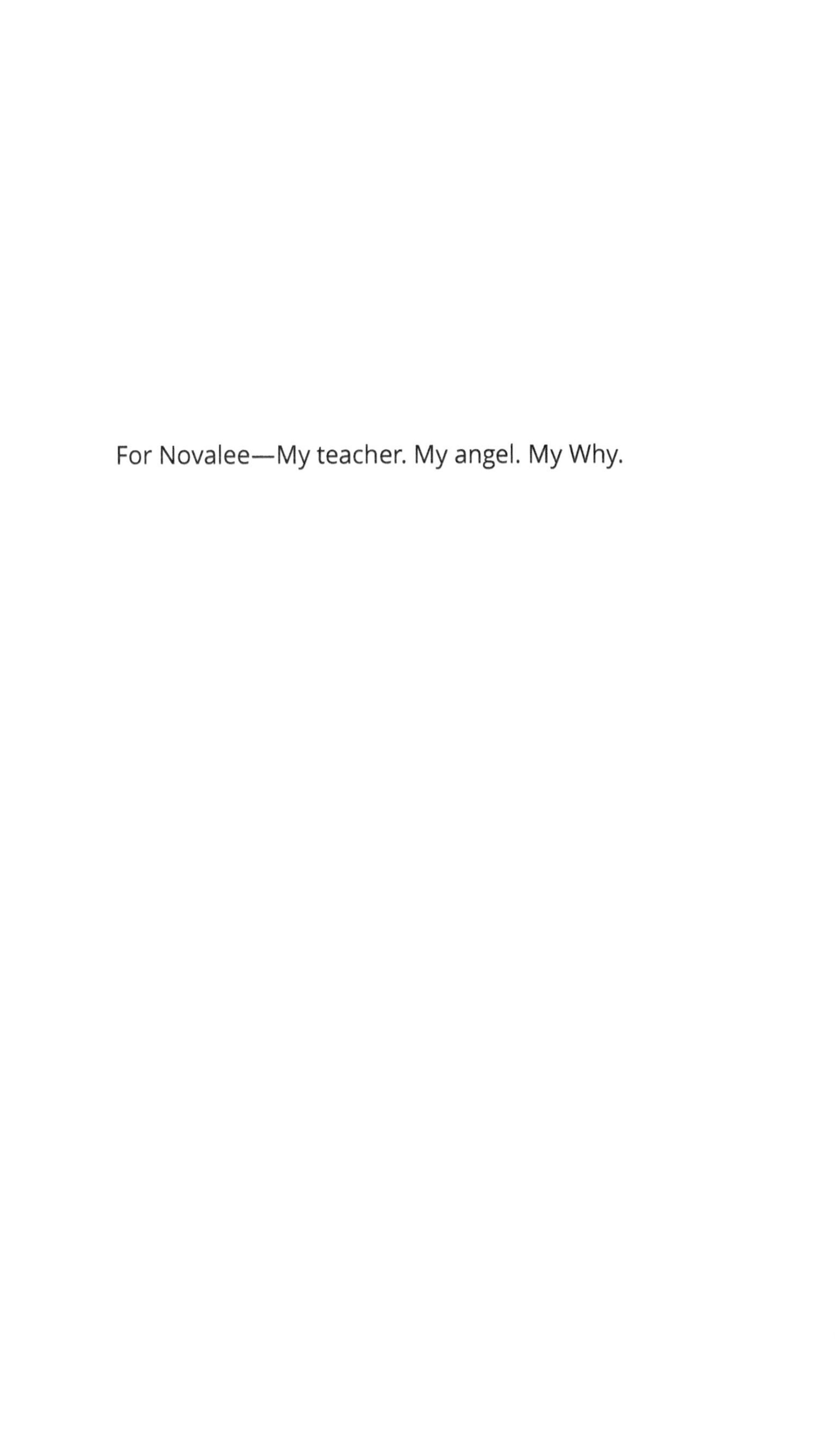

For Novalee—My teacher. My angel. My Why.

A Note Before You Begin

This book isn't stamped with approval from the institutions that are failing our kids—and that's exactly the point.

It wasn't written by someone with ten letters after their name. It was written by someone who's lived it, studied it, tested it, and seen it work in the real world.

You won't find traditional credentials here. You'll find clarity, a mind built for solving problems differently, and the missing instructions most professionals were never taught.

This isn't here to replace professional advice. It's here to challenge it—and to offer another way forward.

If that feels uncomfortable, lean in. Change always is.

Table of Contents

Prologue

For the ones who feel it but can't explain it.

Something feels off.

You can't always name it. You can't always see it. But you feel it.

You feel it in the people around you. In the systems we've created. In the way we've learned to numb, distract, or pretend.

There's something we're not talking about.

Something underneath the stress and anxiety and burnout and violence.

Something we're all quietly carrying but never taught how to unload.

This isn't a book about symptoms.

This is a book about patterns.

About what happens when we are never shown how to understand our minds, regulate our emotions, or rewrite the internal scripts driving our lives.

What follows is a story. And once you see it clearly, you'll realize how many people it could belong to.

Throughout this book, I speak directly to mothers—not because others aren't important, but because I needed to write to the version of myself that would call out the fiercest part of me. This isn't about being a mom. It's about being someone who has something worth protecting—and being willing to burn down what needs to go in order to protect it. If you are simply someone who gives a damn—please know: this message is yours too.

Turn the page.
There's something I need to show you.

Part 1
The Why

*Because when your why is big enough,
everything else tends to fall into place.*

—Peter Sage

The bathroom light flickered against the mirror, casting sharp shadows across my face. My breath was steady—too steady. My hands didn't shake. I wasn't crying. I wasn't panicked. I wasn't anything at all.

I opened the medicine cabinet and let my fingers trace the smooth, cold bottles lined up inside. It didn't matter which one I grabbed. It didn't matter how many I took. The goal was the same.

I wasn't thinking in the way people expect. There was no dramatic moment of doubt, no hesitation, no desperate last-minute plea for help. Just exhaustion. A deep, bone-heavy exhaustion that made everything else feel distant, unreal.

I twisted the cap off, tilted the bottle, and watched as the pills tumbled into my palm. Something had been eating away at me from the inside, and it was still hungry, even though I had wasted away into something I could barely recognize anymore.

One by one, I swallowed them. No hesitation. No second-guessing.

I swallowed a pill to take away the loneliness. Another two for the fear and the feeling of never belonging. One for the belief that I was broken, that something was wrong with me. One because I was too much for most and another because I was not enough for others.

More and more for the countless moments of being unheard, unseen, and misunderstood. And the last pill in the bottle for the certainty that nothing was ever going to change.

The weight pressing on me for so long had finally settled, like the moment just before freefall—calm, detached, inevitable.

I didn't think about the future. I wasn't hoping for someone to stop me. I just wanted it to be over.

How long does this take to work??

"Hey," I heard from outside the door. "It's time to go."

Damn. Not soon enough.

Then, like nothing had happened …

I came out of the bathroom, slung my backpack over my shoulder, walked out of the house and got on the school bus.

I was 11 years old.

This isn't just my story—it's an epidemic.

Bark Technologies is a company dedicated to online safety, using AI-driven monitoring to detect potential dangers in children's digital lives, including cyberbullying, self-harm, and suicidal ideation.

Their 2024 Annual Report on Children and Technology analyzed nearly 8 billion online activities of children, including text, email, and 30+ apps and games that feature a "chat" function—uncovering alarming trends in youth mental health.

The data shows that almost 37 percent of tweens and nearly 60 percent of teens were involved in situations related to self-harm or suicide.

This crisis is real. These aren't just numbers—these are real children. Your children. Hurting quietly. Drowning in emotions they don't know how to name, let alone escape.

Some are bullied for their race. Others for their gender identity, their bodies, their neurodivergence, their poverty, or the way they process the world. It doesn't always look the same, but the pain it causes runs deep—and it often goes unnoticed until it's too late.

And too often, just like me, they feel like they have nowhere to turn.

Like 14-year-old Adriana, who was relentlessly bullied and attacked at school in New Jersey. The humiliation was too much. She took her own life.

Like 12-year-old Drayke, who lived in Utah. He was bullied to the point of no return. His parents found him in his bedroom, where he had hung himself with his favorite hoodie.

Like the thousands of children whose pain goes unseen—until it's too late.

Like the girl who sat perfectly still in class, never made a sound, and still somehow got labeled "a distraction." Like the boy who made everyone laugh because it was easier than asking for help. Like the nonbinary kid whose eyes stopped shining the moment their name became a joke in someone else's mouth. Like the high achiever who smiled on the outside while mentally rehearsing her own eulogy every night before bed.

All the kids who didn't die but quietly stopped living.

Even now, I don't have the right words to fully describe it. How do you explain a pain so deep it hums beneath your skin? A weight so dense it presses the air from your lungs? A silence so wide it starts to swallow your sense of self?

But if you want to come as close as possible to understanding—put on the song "Hide and Seek" by Imogen Heap. Sit still. The vibrations drag you under, like slow motion in a dream.

At first, it's tender—almost pure. But then, you hear it: The echo that doesn't quite come back right. Bent notes wrapped in velvet, laced with resignation. It doesn't scream. It doesn't fight. It just pulls.

Like a siren calling you home—not to safety, but to silence.

And you welcome it. Because surrender feels like mercy.

Let it wash over you now, as you imagine you're 11 years old.

Imagine waking up every morning with a pit in your stomach. A feeling you don't have the words for. It isn't just sadness. It isn't just fear. It's something deeper. A kind of exhaustion that makes every movement feel heavy, every task overwhelming, every moment unbearable.

Imagine knowing—without a doubt—that something inside you is broken. That no matter what you do, no matter how hard you try to be what they want you to be–you will always fail.

You don't know why you feel this way. No one has explained it to you in a way that makes sense to you. No one has given you tools you can use to manage it.

Instead, you're told that your brain is defective. That you were born this way. That your emotions are nothing more than a chemical imbalance that can only be fixed with pills.

Mind-numbing, side-effect-ridden pills.

Imagine carrying a sadness so heavy it makes you feel sick. But instead of help, you are met with punishment.

You miss school—not because you don't care, but because your body refuses to move. You are frozen in bed, staring at the ceiling, willing yourself to get up, to be normal, to be good.

But you can't because you are terrified of what awaits you there.

And so you are punished. Detention. Grounded. Another lecture. More disappointment.

You lash out—not because you want to, but because the anger and frustration have nowhere else to go.

But no one asks why. No one wonders what is happening beneath the surface. You are sent away, told to behave, made to feel like you are the problem.

Like you had any other choice.

Imagine standing in a crowded school hallway, screaming inside, but no one notices. Imagine sitting at the dinner table, feeling invisible.

Imagine the unbearable truth sinking in: No one is coming to save you.

Now, imagine at 11, standing in the bathroom, staring at all the pills in your palm.

Imagine tightening a makeshift noose around your neck or holding a gun to your head.

Imagine believing, with everything in you, that the only way to make it stop—the only way to finally be free of the pain—is to die.

Because at this moment, the pain of living outweighs the fear of dying.

Imagine this is your child.

Like 10-year-old Izzy, a bright and creative young girl who lived in Utah. When she was bullied relentlessly for her race and socioeconomic status, she cried out for help, but no one listened. Her mother found her lifeless body in their home. She had taken her own life.

Like 12-year-old Hayden, in Texas, who died by suicide just days before his birthday. His parents said he was struggling with isolation and despair, feelings that so many kids face in silence.

For many children, the pain is not just emotional—it's physiological. They are overwhelmed, their nervous systems hijacked by fear, loneliness, and hopelessness. And yet, we still expect them to navigate life without the tools to understand or regulate what they're feeling.

✦ ✦ ✦

They said I was mentally ill.

Not traumatized. Not dysregulated. Not terrified. Just diseased ... broken.

I was handed diagnosis after diagnosis; an alphabet soup of disorders meant to explain away what no one bothered to understand. The names kept changing—major depressive disorder. Refractory depression. Bipolar II. Atypical depression. Double depression.

And with every new label came another prescription. Another pill. Another silent message: Your pain is a pathology. Your emotions are the enemy. You are the problem.

I remember one night. I was 12, refusing to take my meds. I didn't like how they made me feel—numb, dizzy, disconnected from myself.

My mom and I got into an argument, and it escalated fast. She ended up pinning me to the floor between the kitchen and living room, straddling my chest, screaming at me to open my mouth.

"You need to take these! Your brain is broken!"

I was thrashing, crying, trying to push her off, but she just kept trying to shove the pills down my throat.

That moment didn't just break my trust in her—it broke my trust in myself.

The message was clear: My feelings were not valid. My resistance was not allowed. My body was not mine.

"Your brain is BROKEN."

That phrase became a scar. It echoed inside me for years, until it stopped sounding like my mom's voice and started sounding like mine.

That night left a permanent imprint—a baseline sense that I was unsafe not just in the world, but inside my own skin.

No one ever looked beneath the behavior. No one wondered if maybe my brain wasn't broken, maybe it was trying to protect me from a world that felt unsafe.

We don't give children the language to understand trauma. We give them pills to silence it.

These kids are not anomalies. They are not outliers. They are the heartbreaking proof of a system that is failing them.

And worst of all, the crisis isn't improving—it's escalating.

Internal turmoil is beginning to rapidly and violently erupt outwards.

For many, the moment that changed everything was April 20, 1999, a day that shook the nation.

Two seniors at Columbine High School in Colorado, Eric and Dylan, walked into their school armed with guns and homemade explosives. They murdered 12 students and a teacher before turning their weapons on themselves.

It was one of the deadliest school shootings in history at the time, and for many, it was the first exposure to this kind of unimaginable horror.

But it wasn't the last. Far from it.

A study published in the *Journal of the American College of Surgeons* in April 2024 analyzed 2,056 school shooting incidents involving 3,083 victims between 1970 and 2022.

It found that the number of school shootings has increased annually from a mere 20 incidents in 1970 to 251 incidents by 2021, and nearly two-thirds of the shooters were under 17 years old.

Each incident is a grim reminder that we are failing to address the root of the problem. Bark Technologies's report correlates with this observation that the internal turmoil many kids are dealing with is becoming more outwardly violent, finding that 72 percent of tweens and 82 percent of teens are digitally expressing thoughts or being exposed to subject matter of a violent nature. Increased violence at schools isn't limited to gun violence, either.

On April 21, 2016, Amy, a female 16-year-old student in Delaware, was attacked by three other female students in the second-floor restroom of the school. Dozens of other students watched the attack, and it was recorded on at least two cell phones. Once the beating was over, Amy lost consciousness. She was pronounced dead shortly after her arrival at the hospital.

These tragedies don't happen in a vacuum. They happen in a system that fails to support kids before they reach their breaking point. A system that punishes instead of helps. That silences instead of listens. That waits until it's too late, then wonders why.

Not every child ends up in a grave.

Some end up in gifted programs, hiding their pain behind straight As and people-pleasing themselves into doormats.

Some end up in detention halls, labeled defiant and aggressive when really, they're drowning in unspoken grief.

Some end up dissociated—floating through life like ghosts.

These are the kids who learned to mask. Who smile in public and fall apart behind closed doors. Who adapt just enough to survive, but never feel like they truly belong anywhere.

They are the high-functioning anxious achievers. The class clowns. The loners. The caretakers.

The ones you'd never suspect.

I was considered a delinquent. Silent panic attacks kept me from school almost daily, though at the time I had absolutely no idea what they were or what was happening to me.

Every other weekend, like clockwork, we'd be driving back to my mom's house and pass the sign for the juvenile detention center—it was literally our exit. There was a sign on the highway just before it, pointing drivers to turn off if they were headed that way.

Without fail, every single time, my dad would point and say loud enough for all of us to hear, "And that's where we'll be dropping off Sarah soon if she doesn't start behaving."

I was 13 when it started. And he kept saying it. Every other weekend. For months.

At some point, it didn't feel like a threat anymore. It felt like a prophecy.

I stopped wondering if I was a bad kid. I just started accepting that I was. People didn't believe me when I would tell them I felt frozen and unable to talk. To them, I was just being a jackass teen who was ditching school.

Schools don't know how to handle pain. They're built to manage behavior, not emotions. To control, not connect. When a child shuts down, lashes out, or falls behind, the system responds with detentions, suspensions, expulsions—treating trauma as if it were defiance.

As if fear and sadness are choices kids make on purpose just to be difficult.

But fear doesn't teach safety.

Shame doesn't teach self-worth.

The very places where children are supposed to feel safe have become sources of more trauma.

The truth is, I never left the house. I lived vicariously through TV and movies and PBS documentaries. But by 13, I had missed so much school that the courts got involved. I remember the day of my court hearing like it was yesterday.

I stood there—meek, tiny, barely 75 pounds soaking wet—in the center of that cold, echoing courtroom. I was quiet, reserved, trying to disappear into myself. But I couldn't. Not with every eye in the room locked on me. My legs felt weak, my breath shallow. I'm sure I looked exactly how I felt: like a deer in headlights, frozen in terror.

The judge walked in, his robe sweeping behind him à la Professor Snape, and he looked me up and down like I was dirt beneath his feet.

"You are a useless human being. I should do the world a favor and throw you into juvie."

I could barely process the words. My heart pounded in my ears, my throat so tight I could hardly swallow.

Lucky me—he was feeling generous. One more chance. My sentence?

House arrest for the entire summer.

"Don't let me see you in here again. Do you understand?"

I tried to nod, but even that felt impossible.

"Don't you know how to speak?"

Somehow, I forced out a yes.

"Not so tough now, I see."

There were adults all around me. Teachers. Doctors. Counselors. Family.

But none of them really saw me.

They saw my silence as disrespect. My panic as attitude. My pain as attention-seeking. My exhaustion as laziness.

I was crying out in the only ways I knew how—but to them, I was just being difficult.

I often wonder how different my life would have been if even one adult had looked at me and said, "This isn't who you are. This is something you're going through."

Just one.

They were too busy asking, "What's wrong with you? Why are you acting this way?" Questions I never had the answers to.

And when they couldn't figure it out either, they made something up and wrote it in my file. They created a version of me that fit their limited understanding so they wouldn't have to confront their own limitations.

No one stopped to think that maybe my behavior wasn't defiance—it was grief. That maybe I wasn't lazy—I was dissociating. That maybe I wasn't manipulative—I was scared.

The system never once stopped to consider that I might be in pain. That I might not know how to do anything about what was happening inside of me.

And if I thought school was unbearable before, that was nothing compared to what came next. Once the kids found out about the house arrest, half of them were afraid of me. The other half wanted to prove they were tougher—because apparently, I was someone "not to mess with."

It didn't exactly make returning to school any more inviting.

My only saving grace? This was the '90s. No smartphones. No social media to immortalize every mistake. My worst moments weren't recorded, shared, or turned into weapons against me.

Kids today aren't so lucky. According to the Barks Technologies report, a whopping 71 percent of tweens and 77 percent of teens have been involved in bullying, whether as victims, witnesses, or even the bullies themselves. And their worst moments don't end when the school bell rings.

These moments follow them home, glowing from their screens, replaying over and over.

This isn't just about individual suffering—it's a societal crisis.

Unaddressed childhood trauma doesn't just disappear. It shapeshifts. Into addiction. Into violence. Into self-destruction. Into chronic illness, broken relationships, and cycles of abuse that stretch across generations.

We are paying the price every single day.

We pay the price in school shootings. In mental health emergencies. In overflowing prisons and underfunded clinics. In parents who don't know how to parent because no one ever showed them how to be safe in their own bodies.

We pay it when we ignore the pain of children and act shocked when that pain explodes outward.

But what if it didn't have to be this way?

What if we gave kids the tools before the trauma turned into tragedy? What if we taught them how their brains work, how emotions move, how to regulate their nervous systems and name their needs?

What if we created a world where kids didn't have to wait until adulthood to start healing?

Because the truth is, we know how to prevent this. We just haven't been brave enough to build it into the system.

Yet.

The years that followed weren't marked by milestones or memories. They blurred together like one long, gray day. I wasn't living; I was enduring.

After age 16, I wasn't considered a delinquent anymore—so I disappeared completely off the radar. But I wasn't better. I was just invisible.

I didn't have many friends. I didn't go out much. I didn't really talk to anyone. I sat in my room while my brother and sister brought me my homework. I read the textbooks. Taught myself. I homeschooled my way through middle school and high school without anyone realizing. Graduated on time with a decent GPA. No one noticed. No one asked why I was never at school.

I wasn't allowed to take driver's ed. I wasn't allowed on field trips. I wasn't allowed to participate in anything that might have given me even a flicker of motivation. Anything that might have helped me feel alive.

That time in my life felt like a fog I couldn't escape. A muted, dreamless sleep I couldn't wake up from.

If you want to understand what that felt like, put on the song "Blur" by MØ. Turn it up loud.

Can you feel the heaviness in your body? The fog in the vibrations? It pulls you through—but so slowly, like molasses. Disorienting in a way that's hard to name.

The song didn't exist back then, but now, every time I hear it, I'm transported back into that silent, aching numbness.

A heartbeat that never sped up.

A life paused but still somehow moving forward.

Like watching your own existence from underwater—or on fast-forward.

I kept waiting. Waiting for someone to notice. Waiting for something to change. Waiting for a sign that I wasn't going to feel this way forever.

But nothing came, and so ... I kept sinking.

Part 2
The How

had my fifth and final suicide attempt at 19. I didn't know why I was still here. I wasn't trying to be saved. I wasn't looking for hope. I just wanted the pain to stop.

But it didn't.

Instead, I was alive—still.

Put on "Help I'm Alive" by Metric. The beat thumps like panic—relentless, erratic. Like being hunted by something inside you. It's not hope you feel. It's pressure.

To move. To survive. To endure.

I was cursed. Cursed to suffer in a world that never made sense to me. Cursed to keep breathing when all I felt was hollow.

Lost. Empty. Powerless.

Alive—but for what?

There had to be a way out. A way to fix whatever was malfunctioning inside me. But the pills weren't working. The therapy wasn't working. Every answer I was given only pulled me deeper into the void.

And now, the warnings on the bottles read like apologies.

"Not suitable for children under 18."

"May increase suicidal tendencies in adults under 23."

Too late for me.

So I made a promise to myself. If no one could tell me how to actually fix my brain, I'd figure it out myself. I was 19. Legally an adult. I didn't have to obey anymore. Not doctors. Not parents. Not anyone. That day, I took back control—or at least, I tried to.

That was the beginning of my quest.

I had just enrolled at the local junior college, College of DuPage a.k.a. "high school with ashtrays," as we called it.

My declared major? Computer programming.

It was logical, practical, emotionless—exactly how I operated. It checked all the boxes my dad had instilled in me: Good money? Check. Job security? Check. Minimal human interaction—my one nonnegotiable. Check.

Perfect.

But every elective, every Gen Ed class I had freedom to choose? I filled with psychology, sociology, anything that might help me understand my own mind.

I spent countless hours hidden in the back corners of the campus library, pouring over dense medical journals while other students grabbed coffee or went to parties. My idea of weekend plans was binge-watching documentaries about the brain, mental illness, and the psychology of serial killers.

It wasn't darkness I was drawn to—it was understanding. I was trying to map the edges of my own chaos.

Eventually, I started sneaking into classes at other colleges—neuroscience, cognitive psychology, human behavior, anything I could find. I hunted down their textbooks and devoured them.

Not because I wanted to be a therapist. Not because I wanted to help other people. That thought hadn't even occurred to me. I couldn't help myself; how could I possibly help anyone else?

I wasn't trying to save the world. I was trying to survive it.

And truthfully, computer science had never been the dream, either. My real dream was buried deep under all the logic and strategy and emotional numbness.

I wanted to move to New York and be on a Broadway stage. I didn't care if I was the lead or just part of the ensemble. I just wanted to be there, in the lights, in the music, in the magic.

There was something about the stage that transcended reality. When the curtain rose, I could disappear and become something more. Something whole. Something felt. Time would stop. Emotion would move through my body like electricity. I could sing until my voice cracked, dance until my legs trembled, and for once, I wouldn't feel broken.

I would feel alive.

But dreams like that aren't built for people like me. I had traded magic for metrics. The stage for a server room. Expression for survival.

And even though I was learning more than I'd ever learned before—about the brain, about trauma, about the way we're wired—it wasn't helping. Not really. My life still felt like a series of silent implosions.

I was unraveling. Quietly. Repeatedly. I struggled just to show up.

College had no patience for my disappearances. If I missed too many classes, I was dropped. If I didn't show up to present, I would fail.

And more often than not, I didn't show up. I was lost, under the covers in my bed and under the weight of the world.

The upside of IT was that you didn't need a four-year degree. The industry moved too fast for academia to keep up anyway. An associate's degree and a stack of certifications was enough.

It spared me the slow, painful death that had been middle and high school.

Eventually, I pivoted into networking. It was less mind-numbing than coding endless strings of ones and zeros. I picked it up fast. Too fast. I would see the patterns, anticipate the problems, fix them before others even recognized them. I didn't just do well—I outperformed entire departments.

But brilliance doesn't spare you from breakdown. Every job ended the same—like a record that couldn't play past track five. A year and a half, maybe two, and I'd unravel. Fired for disappearing. Or I'd vanish first, armed with some polished excuse about moving, or family, or "a new opportunity."

But the truth? My brain had crashed. Again.

My twenties spun like a scratched CD—trapped in a loop of broken relationships, empty promises, and plans that never made it past paper. No matter how much I read, how much I researched, how many answers I hunted down, it never quieted the noise.

If anything, knowledge only made the ache louder. More precise. It showed me what could've been. What should've been. And how far away I was from both.

There was one song I clung to like a flare in the dark: "Time Won't Let Me Go" by The Bravery. You know the drill, go listen.

It starts like memory: shimmering and sad. The beat is nostalgic but restless, like something pacing inside your chest. And when the chorus hits, it breaks.

Wide open. Like longing turned into melody. Like regret dressed in neon and heartbreak.

Each lyric curled around my ribs. The way he sings about wanting to go back, rewrite the past, live the life he missed—it was mine. It echoed the childhood I watched through windows and screens. The laughter I only ever heard secondhand. The adventures I never got to join.

You can't become someone when you've never really been anyone.

You can't find your tribe if you never leave your room.

That song didn't just speak for me. It *was* me. My grief anthem. My secret language. The sound of a girl trying to stitch herself together with movies and songs.

It didn't save me. But it reminded me I wasn't crazy. Just … unfinished.

Still bleeding.

Still looking for the tools.

I had tried almost every prescription out there for depression by this point. All of them were always falling short in some way or making other things worse. Nothing ever "fixed" me. I wasn't cured. I was just in a state of blah. Perpetual blah.

Medication clearly wasn't the solution.

With fire in my chest, I marched into my psychologist's office. I told him, "If you send me out of here with another prescription, I will be dead by the end of the week."

He heard the urgency in my voice. He didn't know I was bluffing, that I believed I couldn't die. That I was cursed to live in this purgatory forever.

"Well," he said, "the next thing would be electroconvulsive therapy. ECT."

"When do I start?" I said, without even letting him explain. Truthfully, I was prepared to take him up on a lobotomy if he offered it at that point.

I just wanted it to stop.

ECT worked. Sort of. I was … lighter. Not healed. Not functional. But something lifted.

I was scheduled for ten sessions. Monday, Wednesday, Friday, for three weeks. Each time, I was sedated, given a muscle relaxant, and shocked into a seizure that supposedly released "happy chemicals."

Even now, it feels surreal: electrocuting yourself in the name of happiness. Something about that just feels off.

It messed with my memory. I wasn't allowed to drive because maybe I would forget how? Forget where I was going? Forget who I was? No one explained much. I was on my own.

And there were the super strange side effects. Everyone I saw looked vaguely familiar. My brain couldn't distinguish between real memories and artificial connections. It made being out in public even more disorienting than usual.

Session ten was supposed to be routine.

"Close your eyes and count backward from ten."

"Ten ... nine ... eight ... seven ..."

And then, blackness. Then—consciousness. But not the kind I was supposed to have.

I could hear them prepping. I could hear the checklist. I could hear them getting ready to administer the shock.

But I was awake!

Awake, paralyzed, and unable to scream.

My heart exploded into panic. My lungs froze. I couldn't move. Couldn't signal. Couldn't do anything but WAIT for it to happen.

I'm screaming inside my mind, *This can't be happening. I have to be in a nightmare. Didn't I see something like this in a movie once? This has to be a terrible nightmare.*

Wake up, wake Up, PLEASE WAKE UP!!!

The heart monitor caught it. It started beeping wildly. They noticed. They acted. Another dose. Darkness again.

I woke up in recovery, still trembling.

That DEFINITELY wasn't the solution.

So I kept searching.

✦ ✦ ✦

That's when I stumbled across something called Transcranial Magnetic Stimulation, or TMS. Like ECT, it stimulated the brain. But instead of electricity, it used magnetic pulses to retrain your neurons to fire at specific intervals. Non-invasive. No sedation. Minimal side effects. You were fully awake and comfortable.

It sounded like something out of a neuroscience fairytale. Maybe it was.

It had just been approved by the FDA. Insurance didn't cover it yet. Only one clinic offered it: Rush University Medical Center in downtown Chicago. The cost was $14,000 for 36 sessions over 6 weeks, 5 days a week.

My family came together and contributed the money. I'll never forget that. I think they were as desperate for peace as I was by this point.

But it worked. At least for a while.

I felt good. Free. No pills. No therapy. Just me—steady, for the first time in years. Two full years. The longest stretch of peace I'd ever had.

And during that stretch, I tried to build a life. I fell in love. Got married. Thought maybe I was finally becoming the kind of person who could settle down, be happy, stay steady.

But I wasn't. Not really. So even though things looked okay on the surface for a while... they weren't.

Eventually, the TMS effects faded. I went back for more. Again. And again. Each round worked less than the last.

Whatever light I thought I'd found flickered, then vanished. Underneath it all, I was still wired for dysfunction.

This was also not the solution.

But something new emerged during those treatments. A whisper. A thread I hadn't followed before.

Meditation.

I read something—one of those random footnotes in a medical article I found laying around the hospital—about how meditation could help reverse symptoms of Alzheimer's. That it could regrow gray matter. It sounded like magic. What if the broken parts of my brain could literally grow back?

So I did what any normal person would do: I flew to Sedona and trained with monks from South Korea to learn meditation.

Wait ... normal people don't do that?

Between the science I was devouring from my books about meditation improving memory, concentration, focus, mood, and the calmness and connection I felt in Sedona, I started to believe maybe—just maybe—there was something to this. Something scientific. Something ancient.

Something real.

Meditation didn't come naturally or easily, though. I struggled. I couldn't "quiet my mind." I couldn't "detach from thought." But I understood it.

Deep down, I recognized what they were pointing to. An internal observation. My real voice. Being connected. And I could feel the energy tingling in my fingers, a small win in my book, in contrast to the others having these huge emotional break-throughs and shifts.

As my time there came to an end, I pulled one of the monks aside. I told him I was scared. Scared that I'd lose the peace I'd found there. Scared that my happiness wouldn't come back home with me.

He looked at me with the kindest eyes and said, "I will tell you the most important thing you must remember."

He paused. "Happiness starts in your feet and is spread through your voice."

Then, he burst into song—Whitney Houston's "I Wanna Dance with Somebody"—and began dancing around outside! (Put it on and dance, you know you want to!)

I looked at him, a very perplexed look on my face, I'm sure. He grabbed my hand and spun me in a circle. I couldn't stop myself from laughing out loud.

Then, he stopped suddenly, placed his hand on my shoulder, and said, "See? Now, you know," and just walked away. Leaving me standing there, completely confused as to what had just happened.

I didn't understand the depth of his words at that moment. But they rooted into me nonetheless. And later, I'd come to see just how profound they really were.

Meditation didn't solve everything. But I finally knew how to get inside my mind—I just didn't know how to fix what I found there.

However, it marked a turning point; a shift. Even as life started unraveling again.

Because it did.

Divorce. Another relationship failed. Another identity shed.

On the day my divorce was final, I left work on my lunch break to sign the papers. I thought I'd feel free. Light. Unburdened after it was all over.

But I didn't feel any of that.

I came back to work, hollow, numb. I sat down at my desk and stared at the computer screen. I couldn't move. I couldn't think.

After what felt like forever, I opened a blank Word document. My fingers started moving. I wasn't thinking about what I was typing. I just typed.

Fast. Raw. Unfiltered.

And when I got to the bottom of the page, I signed my name.

I had written a letter: my letter of resignation.

I think my family thought I was losing it—well, even more than usual—when I just upped and quit my job. No backup plan. No safety net.

I didn't have another job lined up. I wasn't going back to school. I didn't have a strategy. But I had savings. IT had paid decently, and I hadn't spent much—I was always working or researching, anyway. So I bought myself time.

Time to figure myself out.

I was 34, and it felt like I had blinked and lost a decade. Over and over, I asked myself, *How have I still not figured this out? What am I missing? Why am I still failing—no matter how much I learn, how much I try?*

But I didn't give up. I didn't let it consume me.

I'd sit in the quiet with a song on repeat: "Up & Up" by Coldplay. Listen to it now. Something in it kept the belief that there was still a way through. That maybe all the pain, all the spirals, all the restarts weren't wasted. They were part of it.

I didn't know what was next, but I knew it started with the climb back up.

Have you ever had a moment where something completely ordinary ends up changing your entire life?

For me, it was a postcard in the mailbox.

A free week of yoga at a brand-new studio that had just opened down the street. Everyone was talking about yoga. I had never really tried it—not in any meaningful way. The monks had introduced some light movement and basic postures, but nothing like the studio classes I'd heard about here.

I was curious. I had time. I had no job and nothing to lose.

I pulled up the class schedule, browsed through all the descriptions, and landed on one that sounded manageable: Foundations. A beginner-friendly class on Tuesday nights.

Perfect.

I went out and bought a yoga mat. Some stretchy yoga pants. I was nervously excited. Exercise wasn't usually my thing; I found most workouts borderline torturous. And running? If you ever see me running, you'd better run too—because something terrible is chasing us.

But yoga ... yoga seemed different. It had meditation, and that was a language I already knew somewhat, anyway.

Tuesday came. I drove to the studio. Class did not go well.

Then again, I DID sit in my car the entire time so perhaps the data is a bit skewed.

I tried again. Same thing. Glued to my seat, unable to get out of the car.

It took me three Tuesdays to actually get inside that building. *WTF is wrong with me?!*

When I finally made it through the doors, I was okay. A little shaky, a lot nervous—but okay. And like every first-timer, I tucked myself into the safety of the back corner and hoped no one noticed.

The class was challenging. Too many things to think about at once. Breathing, moving, balancing. But it didn't feel like punishment. It didn't feel like gym class. It felt like dancing. Like something familiar. Like something my body already understood.

The instructor came over to talk to me after class. I mentioned that I had studied meditation with monks—you know, trying to be relatable and fit in. She got excited! She recommended I try the restorative class on Thursday afternoons.

So I did.

And after that class, I was hooked.

You walk into a candlelit room. It's quiet, warm, and smells like eucalyptus or lavender—something that makes your shoulders drop before you even hit the mat. There's soft, spa-like music playing. You grab a giant pillow (they call it a bolster, but let's be real—it's a fancy pillow), a blanket, maybe an eye mask. And then ... you lie down.

That's it.

You lie down. And stay there. Sometimes you move into different positions, but slowly, gently. Everything is supported. Everything is held. It's like being tucked in by the universe.

I'm oversimplifying here—there's an entire science to it. A purpose. A structure. Nervous system regulation. Targeted postures for increasing joint and fascia flexibility. But in that moment, it felt like the kind of "exercise" I could finally say yes to.

Yes, please!

✦　✦　✦

Yoga became my anchor. I didn't just practice; I lived it. I was at the studio constantly, trading cleaning hours for unlimited classes, soaking in every moment I could.

I got certified as an instructor. I started teaching and was hired to manage the studio. I built a community of support and friends. And without even realizing it, I had created a world where—for the first time—I felt both calm and capable.

I belonged. I felt purpose in my days. And I was finally beginning to feel ... good.

Things were falling into place. I wasn't just surviving anymore—I was settling into something. I was grounded. Even happy.

Okay, maybe not all the time.

But a lot of the time. Especially when I was at the studio.

So I stayed there as much as I could. Working. Hanging out. Helping with classes. Anything to be near that feeling. That stillness. And I avoided going home or anywhere else as much as possible. I had found a new "bed" to hide from the world in.

But it didn't just feel good—it felt important. Like something I was supposed to understand on a deeper level.

Through my yoga training, I learned more than how to move—I learned how the human body actually works. Not just in pieces, but as a whole. I began to understand how the systems of the body function in tandem, how nothing operates in isolation.

The way we breathe affects the way we think. The way we think affects the way we move. And vice versa. Every part of us is in conversation with every other part, constantly.

Most of us just aren't listening. I know I wasn't.

I learned that even the smallest adjustment in breath can drastically shift your physical and mental health. A few intentional inhales and exhales can pull you out of a panic state. Slow your heart. Refocus your mind. Reground your nervous system.

It's so simple, it almost feels like cheating.

Yoga isn't about stretching. It's about remembering. Remembering that your body is not separate from your mind. That healing isn't linear. That movement is medicine.

And then, there was the yoga philosophy. The element of yoga philosophy that deeply impacted me was the eight limbs of yoga. Think of it like the original personal growth and development manual.

Long before modern self-help books hit the shelves, the Eight Limbs outlined a blueprint for living—how to treat yourself, how to treat others, how to live in integrity with your body and your breath, your mind and your emotions. It was about alignment—physically, but also spiritually. Emotionally. Energetically.

It talked about breath. Purpose. Awareness. Learning to witness your thoughts rather than be ruled by them. Learning to find stillness inside the storm.

It spoke of acceptance and letting go. Living a life of non-judgment.

These were all wonderful things in theory; they made complete sense to me. But no matter how hard I tried, I couldn't apply them to my everyday life. It just seemed so abstract and contradictory to literally everything my brain did.

To the way it seemed the world and everyone in it worked around me.

As I went deeper into my practice, I began training yoga instructors. I started guiding students through their own 200- or 500-hour yoga teacher training.

And it was in that space—that container—that I finally understood what "purpose" really meant, the way it was described in the Eight Limbs.

Yoga teacher training is intense. It's physically demanding. Emotionally confronting. Mentally stretching. It pushes you far beyond your comfort zone in ways you don't see coming. You start the process thinking you're just learning how to teach yoga—but what you're really learning is how to face yourself.

I would watch new students walk in on day one, nervous, uncertain, quiet.

So many of them carrying invisible burdens.

So many of them shrinking inside their own skin.

And I remembered exactly how that felt.

But then, something beautiful happened. Week by week, as I guided them through the material, through the discomforts of growing, I'd start to notice tiny shifts. The way someone answered a question with just a little more clarity. The way their posture changed. The way their breath deepened.

And then, one day, it would click—this spark would light up inside them. And once it lit, it didn't stop.

That glow would grow brighter and brighter until, by the end of the ten weeks, they weren't the same person anymore. They had found their voice. Their center. Their confidence. Their truth.

And every time I witnessed it, it fed a part of me I didn't know was starving.

There's no formula for that. No checklist. No certification that captures it. But I knew—without a shadow of a doubt— that I was meant to help ignite this spark.

That I was here to help empower people.

I had everything I wanted.

I had a job I loved. It didn't feel like work—it felt like purpose. My best friends were also my bosses. The people I managed were like family too. I felt calm, at least, most of the time. Especially when I was at the studio.

It wasn't perfect, but I was content. And that was new for me. I was in a relationship again. And I was pregnant.

It was not an accident. Not a surprise. I had tried. For a year. I had even started down the infertility path with Clomid before it finally happened.

I had always gone back and forth on the idea of having a baby. But at 36, something shifted. That slow-burn ache kicked in—the fear of missing out. What if I waited too long and lost my chance?

It felt like now or never.

And now actually seemed like a good time. I was stable. I had friends and support. Functioning the best I ever had. I'd been working at the studio for over two years without a single spiral. Not even a whisper of collapse.

I was in the best shape of my life. Strong. Grounded. I was teaching yoga, practicing regularly, up until a month before my daughter was born.

I thought I'd just pop her out and be right back at it. I had it all planned.

That was ... dumb.

Because things never go according to plan.

October 2019. Ten days past my due date.

After a long walk through St. Charles Scarecrow Fest with John, my partner, and some family, we headed home and picked up Chinese food on the way.

I ate my veggie spring rolls. My fried rice. Then, I opened my fortune cookie.

"Hope for the best. Prepare for the worst."

I laughed, shocked. "This is the shittiest fortune I've ever received!" I said out loud.

I should have taken it more seriously.

10:30 p.m. The contractions start.

Now, I'd been having Braxton Hicks contractions for the past three months, so this wasn't new. But these were different. Stronger. Deeper. They radiated. They had intention. I knew that this was it.

She was coming.

I texted my doula, Nicki. (PSA: If you're ever having a baby— get a doula. Just do it. You will *never* regret it.) Nicki told me to get in the bath.

"If it's false labor," she said, "the bath will slow it down or stop it."

I got in the bath.

It did not slow down. In fact, it seemed to do the opposite.

Everything sped up. My contractions were now two minutes apart. I could still talk easily—so Nicki told me to hang in there, keep moving, keep breathing. Use low tones. Vibrations. Ground myself.

Yeah, sure. A lot easier said than done.

Around 5:30 a.m., Nicki called again. John answered. I was no longer okay. I couldn't focus. I couldn't talk. She told him it was time—I should go to the hospital.

We were giving birth at the hospital, but I had opted for a midwife instead of a traditional OB. I had planned a water birth. It felt like the calmest option—warm water, soft lights, fewer people staring directly at my vagina.

A win-win-win.

When we arrived, I was already nine centimeters. (I honestly don't know why people feel the need to share this kind of information so freely—but there it is. Do with it what you will.)

It was time. I got in the tub.

Only nothing was happening in the water. Nothing good anyway.

The temperature was dropping. The water was getting cold. I was getting cold.

Nicki gently told me after an hour that it was time to get out. Try a new position.

I moved to the bed. I pushed with everything I had. It wasn't beautiful or empowering. It wasn't anything like the movies.

It hurt. It was not a sensation of discomfort. Not pressure. Pain. Over my entire body, throbbing from my spine to my fingertips.

I wasn't comfortable. I wasn't centered. I was terrified. I don't even know what I was afraid of—maybe something in me already knew what was coming.

Ninety minutes of pushing passed. I was close. Just a few more contractions. Just a few more tries.

Then it hit.

A sensation that wasn't a contraction—even more intense. Raw. Radiating. Seared into my nervous system like a brand. I can still feel it.

I screamed.

I pushed—out of instinct, out of survival—and kept pushing. And pushing. And pushing.

And then—release.

She was out. Novalee Mirren was here.

From the first contraction to birth: ten hours.

Little did I know those were the last ten hours of my life.

Okay—not literally. Obviously, I'm here, writing this. But everything I was ended in that room.

You'll understand soon.

I've seen all the movies and shows. You know the scene: the baby is placed on the mother's chest, she looks flawless, glowing, beaming with energy and joy.

That's what I expected.

My reality? I felt like I was hit by a dump truck.

I could hear everything around me, crystal clear. But I couldn't move. I couldn't speak. My body felt like scattered pieces—unresponsive, disconnected, no longer whole.

They placed Novalee on my chest. I wanted to hold her, to wrap my arms around her. But I couldn't lift them.

I wanted to sit up, to look at her face. But my body wouldn't move.

They started rubbing her down vigorously with a towel. I knew she didn't like it—I could feel it. But I couldn't say anything. Couldn't stop them.

And then came the real fun part of childbirth—the aftermath.

Because giving birth is only the beginning.

Next comes the placenta. Then, comes the checking. And by checking, I mean: The nurse climbs on top of you and performs what I lovingly refer to as the "heart-stomp portion of CPR" directly on your uterus.

Over. And over. And over.

The goal is to measure how much blood your body is releasing. They're checking to see if you're clotting properly. Each time they press, there should be less blood.

You think contractions hurt?

For me, this was so much worse.

Even though I couldn't move or get words out, I was hyper-aware. I could hear everything. I heard the nurse say to my midwife, "There's a lot of blood."

Jennifer, my midwife, came to my side.

"Sarah," she said gently, "we're having a hard time getting your uterus to stop bleeding. I'm going to have the nurse give you Pitocin to help it contract."

I think I nodded. Or maybe I just blinked.

Time passed. More pressing. More pain. More blood.

"It's not working," someone said.

Another medication. More time. More pain. Still bleeding.

"Sarah ..."

My eyes were closed. I hadn't realized it until I heard my name.

"We have one last medication to try. If that doesn't work, we'll have to page OB. If we can't stop the bleeding, they'll need to take you to surgery. They may need to remove your uterus."

All I could focus on was the pain.

Then—someone grabbed Novalee from me. I felt her warmth and weight disappear. I couldn't reach out or say stop.

I was listening intensely.

Her oxygen was dropping. Something was wrong. My body was too broken to react, but inside, every cell was screaming.

They whisked her to the NICU. Nicki looked at John and instructed him to go with her. She stayed with me.

If you ask John what he remembers most from that day, he'll probably tell you, "There was so much blood."

More pain. More pressing. More blood.

So much blood.

"Page OB," I heard Jennifer say. "It's not slowing down."

They rushed me into surgery.

Everyone assumed it was my uterus that was bleeding. It wasn't.

Here's what actually happened. Warning: This is a bit graphic and absolutely way too much information about my lady parts.

As Novalee made her way through the birth canal, the pressure and friction caused multiple blood vessels in my vaginal and perineal region to rupture all at once. The result was a massive internal hematoma—essentially, a large collection of blood pooling beneath the surface inside my body.

Think of the worst bruise you've ever had, then multiply it by about a hundred. Mine was nine by seven centimeters. It was deep. It was hidden. And it was growing.

And that moment—the one where I screamed from pain that didn't feel like a contraction? That was the hematoma ripping open under the pressure of blood pushing out. Like a volcano erupting from the inside of my body.

Once Novalee was out and her pressure removed from the ruptured tissue area, the bleeding accelerated.

I was bleeding to death, and they were looking in the wrong spot for the source.

Novalee knew it. Her little freak out moment, a response to my distress. Her oxygen stabilized without intervention the moment she was out of the room—away from my chest, away from the sound of my heartbeat slowing, my breath fading.

I spent almost two weeks in the hospital. I received blood transfusions and multiple rounds of antibiotics because I kept spiking fevers. I was in so much pain, I could barely move or stand up, let alone walk. John would bring Novalee to see me for an hour or two each day.

It wasn't supposed to be this way.

Even after going home, I wasn't okay. I felt like I had woken up in someone else's body—frail, unstable, wrecked. Like I'd aged fifty years overnight and been dropped into a body that had already lived a hard, painful life. I couldn't move the way I wanted to. I couldn't trust my own legs.

I felt like a prisoner, trapped inside a body that no longer belonged to me, with no way out.

And now, I had a baby. A tiny, fragile human who needed me for everything.

Every time I stood up, I feared I'd collapse. My muscles had wasted away from all the bed rest. There was nothing left to hold me together. My joints were unstable, my hips torn—both labrums shredded, unsupported. My left leg was the worst. It would just buckle beneath me without warning.

And I was terrified. Not for me—for her.

I was scared to carry her. Scared to walk across the room. Scared to pick her up from her bed. What if I fell? What if I dropped her? What if my body betrayed me again—and this time, she paid the price?

I couldn't care for her the way I wanted to. I could barely care for myself. And that grief—of not being able to mother your own child the way you dreamed of—I didn't think anything could feel worse.

✦ ✦ ✦

It was February 2021. Super Bowl Sunday. John came home late and drunk.

He wanted sex. I didn't. I said no, more than once.

He begged, whined, guilted, pressured. He wouldn't let up.

And like so many nights before, even though I was in pain—even though I didn't want to—I gave in just to make the intimate terrorism stop.

But this time was different. I had already taken my sleep gummies. I told him that. His response?

"That's okay. You can sleep right through it. I don't mind."

Yeah. I don't have words for that either.

I wish I *had* slept through it. But instead, I was half-conscious—suspended between sleep and something that felt like assault. I remember finally forcing out the words, "Hurry up," just to get it over with.

When he finished, I locked myself in the bathroom.

Curled up on the cold floor. And cried.

I promised myself: Never again. NEVER again.

But even that vow felt useless. Like screaming into a void.

The next morning, I still made breakfast. Still played with Novalee. Still cleaned the house. Still pretended it hadn't happened.

It would take another week before I saw it clearly. Before I *felt* it fully.

And once I did, I couldn't unsee it.

Novalee was around 18 months old, sitting on the floor by her basket of toys. John had just gotten home from work and stopped to interact with her on his way to the bathroom.

I wasn't paying attention to them at first. But then, I heard something shift in her voice. A subtle distress.

My "mom" ears caught the change instantly, so I looked over.

He had taken one of her toys and was teasing her with it, pretending to hand it back, only to snatch it away at the last second. She got more agitated with each fake out, until after the fourth time, she finally broke.

Screaming. Crying. Overwhelmed.

And then, he said it. "Geez, I was just playing. You're too sensitive—just like your mom."

And in an instant, everything snapped into focus.

It was like someone hit play on a highlight reel of our entire relationship—and every moment I'd ignored or explained away came rushing back at once. I saw it. *All* of it. The pattern. The manipulation. The blame.

I saw it not as a participant this time—but as a witness. I saw how he pushed and poked, then punished the reaction.

For the longest time, I had believed the problem really was me. That I was "too much." But that moment spoiled the illusion. It wasn't me. It was *him*.

This was officially a relationship with an emotionally abusive dynamic.

And now, Novalee was a part of it too.

John was out with friends for the night.

I had just put Novalee down. She wasn't asleep yet—she never was right away. She'd roll around in her bed, singing little songs to herself, her voice rising and falling like waves.

I sat on the couch in the dark, the baby monitor humming beside me. Her soft voice floated in and out of the static. I held my breath, praying she wouldn't call for me.

I didn't have anything left to give.

My body ached. My hips were on fire. My legs were throbbing. I still couldn't move right. I still didn't feel like myself—like I had been permanently separated from my body and dropped into someone else's life.

But worse than the pain was the weight.

I was drained. Emotionally scorched. The kind of tired that makes your soul feel thin. The kind of tired where you stop wanting anything at all. Not food. Not company. Not hope.

Even though it had been a week since that night with John— and just days since the moment with Novalee—it already felt like a distant fracture. One I still hadn't fully dared to face. Everything was heavy and hollow. Like I had died, and my empty corpse was still roaming around in my place.

And that's when it happened.

Through the static, through the darkness, her voice came through the monitor:

♫ You are my sunshine ... my only sunshine ... ♫

I shattered.

I curled up on the couch and sobbed like I had never sobbed before. It wasn't gentle. It wasn't pretty. It was guttural. Animal. The kind of grief that rips open your ribcage and scrapes the inside of your soul raw.

Because in that moment, I started to wonder ... Did I actually die the day she was born?

Like truly die? RIP, dead?

Did all those wishes to be dead—since I was 11 years old—finally come true?

Because I didn't want that anymore!

Not now. Not like this.

This wasn't peace; this was hell.

Not poetic hell. Not symbolic hell. Actual. Fucking. Hell.

And the worst kind, in my opinion—an identical continuation of your life, where you don't realize you're dead, but everything you love gets ripped away from you in the most messed up, soul-twisting ways imaginable.

One domino at a time. My body. My mind. My work. My community. My friends. My purpose. My family.

I was trapped inside a nightmare with no door out. Watching my life collapse in slow motion, unable to intervene.

And through it all, her voice kept singing—this pure, innocent melody floating through the static.

♫ You make me happy ... when skies are gray ... ♫

She was my sunshine.

The only light that cut through the dark.

And all I could think was, *Oh my God ... what if she becomes like me? What if she inherits my dysfunction? What if she lets people mistreat her? Use her? Hurt her?*

What if she's stuck in this darkness one day and doesn't know how to get out? What if I don't fix this—and it kills her?

Because children don't learn what's right by what we say. They learn by what we do.

And by the boundaries we let others trample.

If I let people abuse me, her brain will register that as normal.

And one day, someone will hurt her, and she'll think it's okay. She'll think that's love. And it will be my fault.

That was the moment. Right there.

Rock bottom.

And the turning point. Because as much as I wanted to disappear, as much as every part of me felt drained beyond recognition—I couldn't let this be her legacy.

I had to leave John. I had to rebuild my life. I had to fix my broken brain.

Not to save me.

Not to stop myself from the hurt.

But because suddenly I saw what was really at stake.

I didn't care how long it took. I didn't care how impossible it felt. I didn't care if I had to burn everything down and rebuild it from scratch.

I was going to find a way out, so I wouldn't pass it on to her.

This darkness stops with me.

It was time to open my eyes to the light, and wake up.

The thing about change is, everybody wants their life to be different ... until they realize it means *they* have to be different.

Change is hard.

Change is uncomfortable.

Change is definitely not something that happens overnight.

But when you hit that edge—when you've endured all you can, tried everything you know, and finally realize that staying the same will destroy you and what you love most— something shifts.

A door opens.

And this time, you walk through it.

That's when I started to hear it: the tap of Paul's foot. like a metronome performing CPR on my cold, still heart.

Thump. Thump. Thump.

Steady. Measured.

Then, the melody of "Blackbird" by The Beatles began to play softly along in my mind. The lyrics, like a prayer, breathing life back into my soul.

Go ahead, give it a listen.

Can you feel how it's like the tiniest flicker of life inside a long-dead system—calling you back? Back to the strength that's been buried for so long.

I was waking up. To my pain, to my patterns, to my power.

And finally learning how to fly.

It was subtle. Slow. Uneven. Just like a baby bird, but it was real.

And it started there.

Though I knew I had to change, and things had to change, I still didn't know what exactly to do. Things were uncertain. I didn't know how to get out of my marriage—it wasn't just me anymore. Novalee had to be considered. I had no job, no money. I was still recovering physically.

My first thought was, *I need to become self-sufficient.*

But a typical job wouldn't work for me. I needed something flexible. Something I could do at midnight from my bedroom while everyone else was asleep.

So I started my own bookkeeping business.

I didn't have much experience, but it was logical. Organized. Quiet. I thought it might work. I got a few clients, enough to keep me busy.

But I was exhausted. Disconnected. Forcing myself to chase something that didn't light me up. I was working my ass off and getting nowhere. I wasn't charging enough for the hours I was putting in. I wasn't building toward anything sustainable.

Six months had passed, and I was still no closer to leaving.
Still no closer to freedom.

It was like patching leaks in a sinking boat—I was always drowning.

This wasn't working.

This wasn't helping me.

It was just another trap. Another endless track. Another thing I was supposed to hold together while I quietly broke behind the scenes.

I felt stuck. Defeated. Spinning in circles trying to save myself with magic beans I hoped would grow into something.

I didn't want more chaos.

I wanted meaning. I wanted change. I wanted a solution.

And that's when I found Peter.

That's when I found EMF.

It was probably a 2 a.m. spiral. I was on Facebook, most likely trying to numb myself.

I know it sounds weird, but I actually use Facebook for ads. I'll literally say out loud what I'm looking for, and when I open the app, there it is. It's like my own personal search engine; it saves me the trouble of digging around for options.

Creepy? Yes. Useful? Also yes.

It was especially useful that night because I came across an ad from some British guy named Peter Sage.

He was talking about why we can't change, no matter how hard we try. And that hit me like a punch to the soul. Because that was exactly what was happening. I had been trying—so hard—for nearly two decades, and still getting nowhere.

And Peter?

Well, Peter was ... different.

He wasn't like the other self-help voices I'd heard before—he wasn't "woo-woo," and he wasn't sterile or clinical, either.

He was sharp. Clear. Confident in a way that didn't feel too arrogant, just certain—like he already knew the truth and wasn't here to convince you, just to remind you.

And then, of course, there was the accent.

That lovely British accent that somehow made even the hard truths sound charming and welcoming. But it wasn't just the way he spoke that mesmerized me—it was what he said.

He communicated in my natural language: science and programming.

He explained that your subconscious mind is like a codebase running in the background, silently dictating everything you do. That your external life is just a printout of your internal code.

He talked about subconscious programming, yes, but also about cellular inertia. How even when your mind wants to change, your body might resist it.

How the very cells in your body—trained by years of chronic stress, trauma, and patterning—can revolt against change. Because change threatens familiarity.

And the body clings to what's familiar, what's comfortable, even if it's painful.

No wonder I felt stuck.

He made it make sense. And I knew he was right. He wasn't telling me something new—he was giving context to everything I had already learned but could never execute.

It was like he had taken everything I'd been circling for years—psychology, neuroscience, trauma, meditation, spiritual law—and braided it all together in a way that actually made sense.

And he didn't just promise change; he promised transformation.

Not by adding more to what I was trying to balance, but by removing the interference.

I knew—without a doubt—that I had found what I'd been looking for.

Not only did I sign up immediately to take the program, I also signed up to teach it. Before I'd even started it myself.

That's how confident I was. That's how deeply I felt it.

Like something ancient had finally clicked into place.

And right on cue, Steppenwolf's "Magic Carpet Ride" kicked on in my head.

It was as if Peter reached right through the screen, winked, and said, "Fancy a ride?"

Yes, Peter. I absolutely do.

Grab your headphones and feel the opening bassline buzz through your chest like ignition.

The drums drop—steady and surreal—and you're lifting off the ground.

Nervous excitement tingling through your body as the sound moves with anticipation—like the slow climb of a rollercoaster, suspended at the highest point—just before the drop launches you into the ride of your life.

I knew this wasn't just any old course.

This was my solution.

The first thing that ever explained my mind in a way that actually made sense.

The first time I felt seen—not as a diagnosis, but as someone whole who just hadn't been handed the right instructions yet.

And suddenly it was crystal clear: My brain wasn't broken. It had never been. None of ours are.

We've just never been taught how to use them properly.

And that was the moment everything shifted. From fixing *my* brain ... to helping everyone else realize they're not broken either.

✦　✦　✦

It was the first time in my life my mission moved from egocentric to ethos-centric.

Though, if I'm honest, I don't think I consciously realized that at the time. It was just a knowing. A fire. A sense that this wasn't just for me.

EMF—The Elite Mentorship Forum—is a six-month transformational program unlike anything else I've ever seen.

And I've seen a lot!

It's an intensive deep dive into neuroscience, psychology, and personal transformation—built with intentional structure, accountability, and checkpoints designed to ensure you don't just consume the material, you live it.

What made it so powerful was Peter's brilliance in design.

He didn't try to reinvent the wheel; he masterfully assembled it.

He gathered the greatest breakthroughs from the world's top experts in personal growth, psychology, neuroscience, and human behavior, and synthesized them into one unified framework.

Not just the best of the best, but the essentials, refined and made usable.

All the concepts people usually spend decades chasing down in books, courses, retreats, and coaching programs, woven into a single, cohesive system.

It was like someone had taken the entire field of human potential, stripped away the fluff, and handed me a clear, step-by-step blueprint for transformation.

The owner's manual to becoming a fully aligned, self-aware human being.

It guides you through a complete deconstruction of the self—peeling back the layers of conditioning, trauma, and outdated beliefs that have been quietly running your life in the background. And then, it helps you rebuild—deliberately, consciously, and in alignment with who you truly want to become.

There's more to it than that, of course. But you get the picture.

From day one, my mind was blown.

It was like every dot I'd ever collected finally connected. All the loose threads in my mind—scattered, ungrounded— started weaving into something whole as we moved through the modules.

It was laid out simply and clearly. But I'd be lying if I said it was easy.

Going through EMF was, without a doubt, one of the most challenging things I've ever done. I had to take a long, honest look at myself under a microscope.

Every flaw. Every excuse. Every ugly truth I had been avoiding or justifying.

No hiding. No bypassing. No skipping ahead.

I had to face radical truths, parts of me I wasn't used to accepting. And maybe even harder than that, I had to get crystal clear on what I actually wanted.

Not what I was *supposed* to want.

Not what would look good on paper.

What *I* wanted. For myself. For my life. For my future.

I wanted to quit more than once. But I didn't. I couldn't.

Something in me kept going. Kept pushing. I knew I was close. Close to the other side where things would be better.

And once I got there, the view was spectacular.

There wasn't just one breakthrough moment in EMF. There were hundreds. Quiet ones. Loud ones.

Moments when puzzle pieces clicked into place so fast, I couldn't keep up.

Moments when I had to pause the video and just breathe.

Moments when I cried—not because I was sad, but because I was finally starting to understand myself and my brain. For the first time ever.

Piece by piece, the picture got clearer.

I wasn't broken. I wasn't failing. I was finally learning exactly how I work. I had the owner's manual—to me.

Find the song "Lease on Life" by Andy Grammer.

Play it loud. Let the beat move through you—fluttering, fizzy, alive. Like a smile radiating from inside your whole body and spilling out into everything around you.

Because that is exactly what it felt like: a lift. A lightness. Like color flooding into a black-and-white world. Like laughter echoing through ears that had only ever known silence.

And suddenly, I just knew: Everything was going to be okay.

Not because someone told me. Not because I hoped it would be.

But because I could feel it in my bones. In my breath. In the way my body finally stopped bracing for impact.

It was like my entire nervous system whispered, *We're safe now. We made it.*

So, what was it that I actually wanted for my life?

The whole time I was going through EMF, one question kept clinging to my mind: Why don't they teach this stuff to kids?

I asked everyone in the program—other participants, the staff—I even sent the question directly to Peter Sage himself.

"Do you have plans to adapt EMF into a program for kids?"
His answer? "I do not."

He said it wasn't his mission, and I couldn't understand it.

Peter always talked about solving problems at the source. He used this metaphor often—that instead of fishing bodies out of the water downstream, we need to go upstream and stop them from being thrown in to begin with.

And to me, teaching the principles of EMF to children is going upstream. It's the most direct, most powerful, most preventative solution I can imagine.

Give kids the owner's manual from the start. Show them how to be a fully functioning human before the trauma, before the shutdown, before the destruction.

It would change everything. It would stop the bodies from ever going into the water.

These aren't just abstract concepts—they're the fundamental skills that shape how we experience life. These skills are too important to leave up to chance.

Understanding how our brains and emotions work. How to overcome fear. How to create the life we want.

This knowledge shouldn't be something we stumble upon as adults. It should be taught from the start, so kids don't have to struggle the way they currently are. The way I did. Because this isn't just about education.

It's about PREVENTION.

Preventing anxiety and depression before they seed. Preventing self-doubt before it cements. Preventing all the problems we're seeing now before they even begin.

Leaving this to chance is how we got here. And when you look around, you realize, most people never learn this at all!

Numbers don't lie. Grand View Research reported that the global personal growth and development market value for 2024 was estimated to be $48.4 billion—and it's projected to reach $67.21 billion by the year 2030.

How much did you spend? I know I've made my fair share of contributions.

Books, courses, coaching, workshops, retreats—millions of people are searching for tools to help them feel better, live better, be better.

Why?

Because these skills are essential. They're not luxuries or "nice to haves." They are the missing core of what it means to be a fully functioning human being, experiencing life to the fullest.

They are what everything else is built from: wealth, health, and relationships. They are the tools that allow us to actually put all of the "knowledge" we currently learn in school to good use.

If these principles weren't so important, adults wouldn't be spending billions trying to figure them out after the damage has already been done.

And yet, we still don't teach them to children.

Peter always said he never copyrighted EMF because he wanted people to go out and share these principles with the world.

And for that, I'm truly grateful.

During EMF, I came face-to-face with my real purpose. My dream, my vision, my legacy.

I want no child to feel as lost and alone as I once did. I want them to have the tools, the support, and the understanding I never had. So I made it my mission to take everything I learned in EMF and through all of my searching over the past 20 years—and everything I wish I'd known as a child—and turn it into a curriculum.

A real, practical, engaging, age-appropriate framework that teaches kids how to be human. Fully functional, emotionally intelligent, self-aware human beings who know how to reframe thoughts, regulate emotions, and trust their instincts.

My vision is to see this in every school in America—and beyond.

To raise a generation who doesn't have to unlearn decades of pain. Who doesn't ever feel like suicide is the only way out.

I know I can't guarantee outcomes. No one can.

But I believe—*with every cell of my body*—that if this curriculum were in every school, we would see fewer children lost to suicide. Fewer school shootings. Less violence. Less despair.

Because when kids understand how their brains work—when they have the tools to regulate, to reflect, to express, to *feel*—they don't spiral in silence.

They speak.

They connect.

They heal.

They lead.

I didn't know why I couldn't die all those times. Why I was still alive. I used to think I was cursed. But now I know: This is why.

I realized the reason teaching this to kids isn't Peter's mission ... is because it was mine all along.

I was meant to create this. To speak for the ones who haven't found their voice yet. To give kids the tools adults spend their whole lives searching for.

I used to think everything I went through was just my story. My burden. My battle. My brokenness. But the further I went on my healing journey, the more I realized—it happens to all of us.

It's found in children who grow up never feeling safe, seen, or understood. Who then become adults carrying anxiety, depression, shame, and silence, trying to function while still fighting invisible wars inside their own minds.

We've normalized dysfunction.

We've normalized the $40 billion self-help industry trying to fix what was never taught in the first place.

And it's not just the kids who are struggling.

It's the teachers. It's the parents. It's the systems built on survival and suppression instead of awareness and empowerment.

We're all playing out patterns we didn't create—patterns we inherited.

And that's why this work matters. Because this cycle doesn't have to continue.

We can stop it. We can change it.

Not someday—now.

I'm not just building this for the future.

I'm building it for her.

Part 3
The What

Enter: The Life Science Curriculum.

It's not worksheets and lectures. It's not theory kids forget after a quiz.

This is a 36-week transformational journey designed for all levels, from K to 12. It blends science-backed principles with creative activities, breathwork, movement, and reflection. It's designed to help kids build confidence, regulate emotions, understand their brains, and actually *use* that understanding in their everyday lives.

Each week builds on the last. And by the end, students complete a creative legacy project that expresses their transformation, and invites them to share their light with the world.

We explore thought, emotion, goals, relationships, and values—all through the lens of our different brainwaves.

Because the truth is, by the time a child is seven years old, most of their core beliefs about themselves and the world are already set in place.

Why? For the first six to seven years of life, the brain is primarily in a theta wave state—a highly impressionable, imaginative state that absorbs everything as truth. It's the same brainwave adults enter during hypnosis, deep meditation, or when they are dreaming.

In theta, the brain doesn't question. It doesn't evaluate. It just downloads.

So when a child hears, "You don't deserve it." "Stop being so overdramatic." "Why do you always have to make things harder?"

They don't pause to ask: Is that true? Is that even about me? They absorb it as fact.

They don't yet have access to alpha brainwaves—the kind that allow for reasoning, analysis, and self-reflection. They literally can't question what they're being told. The prefrontal cortex—the part responsible for reasoning and decision-making—hasn't matured yet.

So, whatever gets installed in theta often becomes the subconscious operating system carried into adulthood.

And most people never revisit that early programming.

That's why we teach this work early, and revisit it often. So that students aren't just learning about the world; they're learning how their own minds were shaped by it—and how to reshape those patterns when they no longer serve.

Yoga, meditation, and breathwork are also integrated as grounded, practical tools for focus, calm, and resilience.

Let me pause here for a second.

There's a common belief that meditation and yoga are religious. They're not. They can be. But they don't have to be. They're like singing.

Singing can be religious, but it's not inherently so. Neither is silence. Or breath. Or movement. Or stillness.

I'm fairly certain that last year, a mother pulled her child out of Novalee's Montessori school because she found out they were teaching the kids mindful meditation exercises to help them with stillness and being calm and thought it went against her religion.

That broke my heart. Not because of the choice—but because of what it reveals.

What's more, a yoga instructor friend of mine once told me that when she worked as a teacher's assistant at a local church preschool, she was allowed to wear yoga pants—but only if she called them "athletic pants." Because apparently the word "yoga" is banned to use in the church.

Ummm ... what?

Ironically, almost every major religion includes some form of meditation. Catholic rosary beads? Modeled after Buddhist mala beads. Repetitive prayers? That's chanting.

Stillness. Breathwork. Rhythmic repetition. These are ancient meditative tools that have been repurposed in nearly every culture, to quiet the mind, regulate the body, and connect to something greater.

You choose the intent.

And while most religions don't explicitly include yoga as we know it today, many do include ritual movement that mirrors its core elements: kneeling, bowing, placing hands in prayer, prostration, lifting the arms—gestures practiced in rhythm with breath and intention.

That's really what yoga was always about—getting the body, breath, and nervous system working together so you can actually be still. It wasn't about worship, handstands, or hitting a fitness goal.

The postures were originally tools to help people sit longer in meditation, move energy, and stay present in their own body.

Over time, more poses got added—some from traditional lineages, some from other movement practices—to help keep the body mobile and strong in all the ways daily life used to take care of before we all started living like Wall-E—getting rolled around in chairs while machines do the moving for us.

So if you think meditation or yoga go against your beliefs, I'd gently suggest that you might already be doing them. The names are different, but the essence is the same.

Rest assured, the reason they're included in this curriculum has absolutely nothing to do with religion.

They're here because of what science now confirms: These practices regulate the nervous system, improve focus and memory, enhance emotional control, and strengthen overall cognitive function. They help kids learn better, feel better, and live better.

Period.

No belief system required. Just breath, movement, and awareness of your surroundings and your self—used as tools to support healthy, thriving brains and bodies.

And with all of these tools combined, kids walk away knowing themselves.

Like, really knowing themselves.

Because when you know who you are, you stop reaching for who you're not.

And that kind of knowing doesn't come from a single breakthrough. It's built through experience, through repetition.

Each year, students come back to the curriculum with new perspectives, deeper awareness, and a stronger sense of identity. The material grows with them—becoming more solidified each time, so by graduation, they don't just "know" it. They live it. I'll explain more on this later.

Along the way, they discover how to stay strong when everything around them shakes. They develop self-trust that doesn't wobble in the face of rejection. They become thinkers, feelers, and leaders—not because we told them to, but because they now know how to rise, not react.

In a world where kids are drowning in noise, pressure, and performance metrics, this curriculum gives them something school never taught them: how to master their minds, trust their voice, and know what it feels like to come home to themselves.

The Life Science Curriculum isn't just a collection of lessons—it's a developmental arc. There are three phases. Each phase is carefully designed to meet students exactly where they are, then guide them forward with intention, clarity, and care.

This is not linear memorization. It's a journey of expanding awareness, self-discovery, and mastery.

The phases work together to move kids from confusion to clarity, from reaction to self-leadership, and from emotional chaos to purpose-driven living.

Phase 1: Self-Discovery & Mental Mastery

Lessons 1–5

This phase lays the foundation. It helps students understand how their minds work and how their beliefs, thoughts, and emotions shape their experience of life.

Most kids have never been taught how to think about thinking—how to challenge limiting beliefs, or how to recognize that stress, fear, and frustration are not permanent states, but messages from the body and mind. In this phase, students begin to take their power back. They learn that awareness is the first step to transformation.

We focus on perception, emotional regulation, belief systems, resilience, and relationships. It's about helping students see what's really going on inside their minds and lives—and giving them tools to shift it.

Phase 2: Conscious Creation & Personal Power

Lessons 6–9

Now that students understand how their minds and emotions operate, it's time to get intentional. In Phase 2, we explore identity, authenticity, goals, and the internal compass that guides decision-making. Students learn how to tune into their values, align with their truth, and take aligned action.

They build the courage to break out of people-pleasing patterns. They learn how to hold a vision for the future. And most importantly, they start becoming the kinds of people who can create it.

This is where confidence takes root. Students move from self-awareness into empowered self-leadership.

Phase 3: Transcendence & Legacy
Lessons 10–13

This final phase is about integration, expansion, and contribution. Students begin to see themselves not just as individuals, but as creators. They explore consciousness, energetic alignment, and what it means to live a legacy—not someday, but *now*.

They look at the impact they want to have. They reflect on their transformation. They rise into a higher level of responsibility—not because someone told them to, but because they *feel* the truth of their own power.

This phase culminates in a personal legacy project. It is creative. Reflective. Personal. And most importantly, it marks the point where the curriculum becomes *theirs*.

Because by the end of this journey, they aren't just students. They're leaders of their life.

Not perfect. Not finished. But fully aware. Fully alive—and ready to create their world with intention, integrity, and heart.

You've seen how this all came together. Now, here's what it looks like in action.

The Life Science Curriculum includes 13 core lessons, each one designed to build skills, insight, and self-leadership.

Together, they guide students from awareness to action to full embodiment.

The lesson summaries below give you a sense of the flow—and the transformation that unfolds across the year.

Lesson 1: Expanding Awareness & the Learning Journey

Theme: *Understanding how reality works—physically and energetically—and how mindset shapes perception*

Takeaway: You can't change what you can't see.

This first lesson cracks open the door to a completely new way of seeing the world. Kids learn how their minds filter reality, how open-mindedness affects learning, and how both science and energy help explain the invisible forces that influence what we experience. This lesson is foundational, setting the tone for curiosity, critical thinking, and conscious creation.

Lesson 2: Mastering the Mind & Unlocking Potential

Theme: *Mastery, identity, and meditation as tools for personal growth and self-awareness*

Takeaway: When your brain groans, it's growing.

We go deeper into how the brain learns and grows—and how identity plays a role in lasting transformation. Students explore the stages of mastery, the neuroscience behind frustration, and how to shift brain states using music and breath. They also begin reframing internal labels, learning to recognize levels of consciousness, and practicing meditation as a tool for nervous system regulation and insight. Self-leadership begins here—the kids are not just learning what they're capable of, but believing it.

Lesson 3: Redefining Wealth & Abundance

Theme: *Money, value, and the mindset that shapes prosperity*

Takeaway: Gratitude aligns us with abundance. Fear aligns us with lack.

Wealth is more than money; it's mindset, energy, and the ability to create value. Students explore their beliefs around money, challenge scarcity thinking, and discover that true abundance comes from gratitude and contribution. They learn how to approach money creatively, trust in a supportive universe, and practice tools that align their inner world with prosperity. Financial creativity becomes a life skill—and gratitude becomes the gateway.

Lesson 4: Emotional Intelligence & Inner Mastery

Theme: *Understanding emotions, reframing challenges, and regulating the nervous system*

Takeaway: Emotions don't control us, they communicate with us.

This lesson equips students with emotional tools that help them understand, express, and regulate what they feel. We explore the life cycle of emotions, how to name and locate them in the body, and how to process even big feelings without being overwhelmed. Yoga, music, reframing exercises, and

perspective shifting become essential tools. Inner mastery
begins by turning toward emotion, not away from it.

Lesson 5: Understanding Connection & Purpose

Theme: Building healthy relationships—with self, time, purpose, and others

Takeaway: When we understand ourselves, we connect more deeply with the world.

We move through three pillars of connection: self, purpose, and relationships. Students build self-love and self-trust, reflect on time as a flow, and examine their beliefs about higher purpose. We explore personal seasons, the role of faith (in self or something greater), and what it means to show up for others with love and boundaries. Emotional growth becomes social wisdom, and connection becomes a conscious act.

Lesson 6: Strengthening Focus & Inner Stillness

Theme: Concentration, breath, and inner dialogue as the keys to clarity and resilience

Takeaway: Focus doesn't come from force. It comes from training.

Students learn that most distractions are internal, not external. Through breathwork, movement, and visualization, they begin strengthening the voice of their inner champion—the part of them that promotes growth, effort, and resilience. Tools like box breathing, time-blocking, and mindful self-talk help them experience focus as an embodied skill. With each practice, concentration builds—and stillness becomes a source of power.

Lesson 7: Discovering & Living Your Truth

Theme: Authenticity, self-acceptance, and aligned decision-making

Takeaway: You're already whole—the goal is to live like it.

Authenticity becomes the compass in this lesson. Students learn to let go of external validation, forgive themselves and others, and stop chasing feelings disguised as achievements. They explore decision-making from the heart, reframe perceived imperfections, and begin walking their truth with humility and confidence. Self-expression becomes a tool for alignment, rather than simply a performance.

Lesson 8: Goal-Setting with Purpose & Alignment

Theme: Vision, growth, and inspired action through "through-me" thinking—learning to work with *life, not just* on *it*

Takeaway: Goals aren't just about outcomes, they're about who you become in the process.

Here, students reframe goal setting as a journey of alignment and transformation. They learn to focus on how goals feel, trusting inner signals over rigid plans, and balancing big vision with small, actionable steps. With clarity, gratitude, and presence, students begin crafting goals that stretch their potential and strengthen their connection to purpose.

Lesson 9: Archetypes & Identity Evolution

Theme: The inner roles we play—and the power to choose who leads

Takeaway: When the Sovereign leads, the whole system thrives.

We introduce four inner archetypes—Warrior, Lover, Magician, and Sovereign. Students reflect on when these energies show up, which ones dominate, and how to choose leadership that's intentional and values-aligned. They explore the tension between light and dark within each archetype and practice embodying maturity, courage, and balance. Identity becomes a conscious expression, not a default pattern.

Lesson 10: The Mind's Perspective & Thought Patterns

Theme: Perception, beliefs, and the power of intentional thinking

Takeaway: Your thoughts shape your experience—and you get to shape your thoughts.

Students learn how their experiences shape beliefs, how beliefs shape values, and how values shape behavior. We explore how to shift from blame to ownership, rewrite internal scripts, and question automatic reactions. The result is increased self-awareness, emotional clarity, and a growing sense of agency. Thinking becomes a tool, not a trap.

Lesson 11: Defining & Aligning with Core Values

Theme: Values, beliefs, and designing your internal compass

Takeaway: You get to choose who you become—starting with what you value.

In this lesson, students intentionally design the values that will shape their future. They create realistic "rules" for experiencing their chosen values and learn to redefine or release the ones they want to avoid. With reflection, ranking, and journaling, students build a custom inner compass—one that's rooted in growth, grounded in clarity, and ready to evolve with them.

Lesson 12: Consciousness & Expansion

Theme: Power vs. force, duality, and the path to higher awareness

Takeaway: The more we raise our consciousness, the more life flows with ease.

This lesson builds a bridge between vibration, emotion, and intention—showing students how these forces shape the way we show up in the world. Students learn the difference between using force and accessing true power, and they explore tools like sound patterns (cymatics), emotional resonance, and consciousness mapping to understand how their inner world influences their outer experience.

Lesson 13: The Story You Tell & Personal Transformation

Theme: Identity, legacy, and the power of intentional growth

Takeaway: Legacy isn't what we leave behind—it's what we live.

We close the curriculum by turning reflection into power. Students revisit the movie of their life—the challenges that shaped them and the limiting beliefs they're ready to outgrow. Forgiveness becomes a key to freedom, and identity becomes a living, evolving story they get to write. Legacy stops being a concept and becomes a lived experience—one based on love, growth, and authenticity.

Legacy Project: Reflecting & Expressing the Journey

Theme: Creative expression, self-reflection, and personal integration

Takeaway: Growth is the real achievement—and your story is your legacy.

This capstone experience invites students to pause, reflect, and creatively express who they've become—not for a grade, not for performance, but for themselves. Through art, writing, music, or presentation, they share their transformation over the year and craft a message from their future self. It's not about being finished. It's about choosing how they'll continue to grow from here.

Because the greatest legacy we leave is how we live.

✦   ✦   ✦

This curriculum wasn't born in a classroom or a boardroom. It was born in survival and refined in healing.

It's about giving kids what they need. What I never had. What most of us never had. And what I refuse to let Novalee go without.

Rather than walk you through all 13 lessons in detail and make your head spin, I'm going to show you a few of them, through my own stories.

Each chapter that follows reflects multiple core principles and tools that are woven into the curriculum. These aren't hypothetical scenarios. They're real moments I lived, stumbled through, questioned, and ultimately transformed from.

They show why this work matters—tangibly and urgently.

And they invite you to imagine what this could look like, both for your child now, and for the person they're becoming.

The One With the School Bus Dress

*A story about awareness, intention,
and my invitation to Hogwarts*

Every spring and fall, there's a children's consignment pop-up near me called Rhea Lana. It's basically a giant, organized thrift event where parents can buy and sell gently used kids' clothes and gear.

To be honest, I've never been a big fan of thrifting—I don't have the patience for chaotic racks and the endless hunt. I usually prefer to walk into a store, grab what I need, and be done.

But with how quickly Novalee was growing, these sales made sense. I could sell what no longer fit and stock up on the next size for a fraction of what it would cost retail.

That spring, I was headed out to the sale alone. Before I left, I gave Novalee a kiss and asked her if there was anything special she wanted me to look for. Without hesitation, she said, "A shirt with a school bus on it."

I paused. I knew that was going to be a long shot. But I told her, "I'll see what I can do. If I can't find a shirt with school buses, I'll find you something better."

The sale was packed, as always. Racks and racks of clothes organized by size and gender—signs sticking up in every direction like little flags marking a battlefield.

I went into task mode, working my way through the 3T girls' racks like a well-trained survivalist: tank tops, pajamas, spring outfits, a few cute dresses. My cart was overflowing with mix-and-match pieces that would make half-outfit changes easy (because, you know—toddlers.)

I was almost finished, down to the last rack in her size, when my fingers grazed something yellow. I stopped. Parted the hangers. And there it was.

A little yellow and gray dress. Covered in school buses.

"No way!" I said . . . a little too loud. Startling the mom next to me.

I stared at that dress like it had fallen out of another dimension. A whole pattern of tiny yellow school buses. In a sea of pint-size chaos and randomness, there it was—the one thing I never expected to find.

I started laughing as Louis Armstrong's voice played in my head: "What a wonderful world ..."

Yes, Louis. Indeed it is.

Now, I'm not saying one of us magically conjured the dress with our mind ... but I'm also not *not* saying that. That experience solidified the new way I was starting to see the world.

It was the first time I truly experienced that the world might be more connected—and more responsive—than I'd ever realized.

The first thing I learned in EMF was the science behind what I had felt that day.

In school, we were taught Newtonian physics: the idea that the universe is a giant machine made of solid parts and predictable rules. In fact, that model is still the foundation of what most kids are taught today.

It works for explaining basic mechanics, but it doesn't account for what happens at the level of energy, consciousness, or—most importantly—human experience.

This is where quantum physics comes in.

It has shown us that reality is far more complex. And far more interesting.

If you compressed all the physical matter—all the atoms and solid "stuff" of every person on the planet, all eight billion of us would fit neatly into a box the size of a sugar cube.

It sounds impossible, but it's real. Look it up if you want; it'll blow your mind.

Atoms, the building blocks of everything, are 99.999999 percent "empty space," or energy. That means what we perceive as solid matter is mostly illusion.

We are walking waves of energy—connected, responsive, and full of potential.

One of the most famous experiments in quantum physics is the double-slit experiment. It's been replicated over and over with increasing levels of complexity, and every time, it shows the same thing: Particles behave differently when they're observed. Just paying attention can change the outcome—and it often does.

Wild, right?

At the smallest level, particles don't act like solid building blocks. They exist in a field of *possibility*, where *observation* influences what actually happens.

Reality doesn't just exist "out there," separate and fixed.

It responds to the observer.

It's like living inside *The Sims*. We, the avatars, think we're just responding to the world around us. But really, we're also helping create it because our subconscious mind is the builder—the one holding the controller—shaping our external life based on our internal settings.

And if the world is fluid and responsive instead of fixed and separate, then everything we've been taught about life deserves to be questioned.

We act like the laws of physics stop at our skin. Like they only apply to planets and pendulums and not to people.

But what if your thoughts had gravity?

What if your emotions were measurable energy fields, like electromagnetic ripples shaping the world around you?

That's not a metaphor. It's physics. And if it's true ... then the way we raise children, the way we teach them to think and feel, isn't just "soft skills."

It's the foundation of their reality.

That's what I felt when I found that dress. It wasn't magic or superstition, it was the field responding to a frequency. A moment of alignment. Of awareness.

A ripple.

A little girl set a clear desire. I held it in my mind—not obsessively, just gently. And somehow, in the most unlikely place, that desire materialized.

And yet, our education system still clings to outdated models.

We teach children that reality is external—separate from them, and unchangeable.

We tell them that life is something that happens to them, instead of something they actively co-create.

We teach kids to follow the rules of only solid, rigid matter, as if that's the whole truth. As if it makes sense to believe that we are the only thing in the universe that operates outside of universal law.

But the truth is, we're mostly made of space. Energy. Possibility.

It's time for science class to catch up—not just with quantum physics, but with what it means to be a conscious, feeling human being.

Because this isn't just about science or physics.

Most people are still living inside that old model of power-lessness. We're taught to react instead of participate. We're taught to believe what we see, instead of realizing we *see through* what we believe.

And when that's the lens you're raised with, questioning anything outside of it feels uncomfortable, even dangerous.

I know because I grew up in that same kind of environment.

If I asked why, I was often met with frustration or silence. The expectation was obedience—not curiosity.

Does the phrase "Because I said so" ring any bells?

But real growth begins when we challenge what we've once accepted without question. When we open ourselves to asking, "What if we've been wrong? What if something has changed?"

And when the people around us stop shutting down our wonder.

That school-bus dress may not seem like a life-altering moment. But for me, it was. It was the first time I saw evidence of a new kind of reality.

The first time I thought, *Wait. Maybe this isn't all random. Maybe I'm not just surviving a script—I'm helping write it.*

And once you start to see that, you can't unsee it.

That's when I started keeping a list of what we called "positive confirmations" in EMF. Tiny wins. Coincidences. Aligned moments. Clues that reality was responding to me—not just happening *around* me, but *with* me.

It became a way to train my brain to stay tuned into the evidence of alignment, even when the big things hadn't arrived yet. I stopped waiting for proof that life was changing and started documenting the moments that told me it already was.

Even the small stuff mattered.

Especially the small stuff.

But here's the thing: The confirmations start small. Sometimes so small, you can easily brush them off as coincidence.

You think, *Maybe I'm just seeing what I want to see.*

But if you stay with it—if you keep planting new thoughts, holding new beliefs, and shifting how you see the world—those tiny ripples start turning into waves.

The outer world begins to reorganize itself around your new inner alignment. And it doesn't just respond to our thoughts—it responds to the energy behind them.

The consistency. The emotional charge. The trust.

At first, I wasn't even sure it was working. I was journaling my "positive confirmations," trying to stay consistent, even when nothing around me seemed to change.

But like Peter taught us, there's a transition period. A gap between the old reality you created and the new one you're calling in.

And if you can hold steady in that gap, it eventually catches up to you.

Things start happening more and more frequently, each one more undeniable than the last.

Because it's not just one big moment. It's dozens of little ones, each one more undeniable than the last.

Like the time I was running late to meet a friend and found myself wishing I had just 10 to 15 more minutes. Moments later, she texted, "Hey, sorry—I'm running 15 minutes behind."

No stress. No rush. Just the universe buying me time.

Or the day I surprised my niece with tickets to *Harry Potter and the Cursed Child*. They weren't cheap, so I bought seats in the very last row—nosebleeds.

I told myself, "It doesn't matter. It's still magic from the top."

When we arrived months later, a staff member pulled us aside and upgraded our seats to the main floor. No explanation. No asking. Just, "Here you go, enjoy."

It felt like a nod from the universe. A quiet, "I see you."

Then, there was the morning Novalee and I were running seriously behind—still 30 minutes away from school, with not enough time to get there.

But I didn't panic. I just breathed and said out loud, "We'll get there when we get there."

No meltdown. No stress catching a red light or traffic. No checking the clock over and over on the drive.

We had fun, we laughed.

And somehow ... we pulled into the parking lot at 9:00 a.m. on the dot. I still don't know how that math worked.

Sometimes it was smaller than that. Like thinking of someone and they'd text me a few seconds later.

Or wanting Novalee to wear a particular outfit for a special outing. I had my hand on the hanger when I stopped. If I suggested it, she'd reject it out of pure principle.

So I let it go. Told myself, "She'll be herself. That's what matters."

The next morning, she came down dressed in the exact outfit I had almost pulled.

No prompt.

No clue.

Just ... aligned. No magic wand needed.

That's when I started dancing. Smiling. Trusting.

And playing the same song on repeat. "Ripples," by Matisyahu. Play it now.

It became an anchor. My reminder that I didn't have to force things anymore. That alignment was real. That resonance was real.

And every time something came back around in my favor—every time life met me with unexpected grace—I'd hit play again.

And I'd let the music wash over me like ocean waves.

Not crashing waves. Not chaotic ones.

But the kind that carry you. The kind you float in.

That soft cymbal shimmer rising in the background, like the sound of something sacred building, just out of view.

The slow back-and-forth of the bass—a steady swell that almost rocks you. Circular. Repeating. Like breath. Like trust.

There's even this underwater humming off to the side. It's faint, like a presence you can feel but can't quite name.

And his lyrics ... they don't demand. They don't fight for attention. They just glide. Rhythmic, soothing, certain.

It's the sound of letting go; of knowing I don't have to force the current—I can move with it. That life is already rising to meet me, if I just stay in flow.

And every time I needed to remember that, I'd hit play again. And float.

It all starts with awareness.

Because before you can change your life, you have to see it differently.

You have to understand that what you've been taught about reality isn't the whole picture.

That you are not a passive passenger of your life—you are the creator.

And once you know that—once you *really* see it—you can't unsee it. You can't go back.

It changes how you walk. How you listen. How you choose and dream. It makes you pay attention to things you used to overlook.

You realize the world isn't just happening *to* you.

It's responding to you.

You're not just surviving. You're participating.

It reminded me of something I saw in the movie *I Heart Huckabees* once. The metaphor stuck with me.

Dustin Hoffman holds up a blanket and says, "This blanket represents all the matter in the universe. Everything. Nothing has been left out."

Then, he raises two fingers from underneath the fabric. "This is you. This is me."

He keeps moving his hands beneath the blanket. "This is my wife. This is the Eiffel Tower. This is a disease. This is a hammer ..."

He's explaining every form, every experience. It's still just the blanket. Still just one thing, expressing itself in different ways.

The point? Everything in the universe is made of the same thing—just showing up in different forms.

And everything you could ever want or need? It's already part of you. Already woven into your design.

You don't have to chase it.

You just have to learn how to *remember* it.

That's what this lesson is about: helping kids see *beneath the surface* of what they've been taught, so they stop thinking of life as a series of disconnected pieces and start understanding themselves as part of something bigger.

Something connected.

Something alive.

Because before kids can master resilience, emotional intelligence, or self-leadership, they need to understand how the world actually works and their role in it.

This is where it begins. Awareness is the gateway.

And everything else we teach builds from here.

The One With the Mediation Meltdown

*A story about the four stages of knowledge, false peaks, and the
time my nervous system laughed in my face*

I had made it. Or at least, I thought I had.

After completing EMF, after weeks of intense personal
breakthroughs, rewiring old patterns, and stepping into what
felt like an entirely new version of myself, the transformation
was complete. I had broken free.

The old me was gone, and a new version of myself was
here to stay.

And then, the universe, in all its infinite wisdom and wicked
sense of humor, let out a deep, satisfied chuckle. Like when my
daughter, with all the authority of a five-star general, tells me
she's going to "make" me do something—tiny hands on hips,
eyes full of conviction, blissfully unaware that she has exactly
zero leverage in this situation.

"Oh, really? You've transformed? That's adorable. Let's see
how that holds up."

It didn't.

I fell flat on my face.

It wasn't all at once. No sudden collapse of everything I had
learned.

Instead, it was stealthy, invasive, slipping back in without announcement. It crawled into the edges of my awareness, many legs pressing against my skin like a centipede seeking warmth in my ear. I didn't notice at first, until it was too deep, too fast, too far inside.

I felt that sickening sensation—the kind that makes your scalp prickle and your stomach drop, knowing something is moving where it shouldn't be.

This Jekyll-and-Hyde realization landed slow and heavy: I wasn't as transformed as I thought.

And then, I heard Peter's voice in my head: "Theory alone doesn't cover the price of admission to higher levels of consciousness."

Yeah, he wasn't kidding.

Have you ever read a book or listened to a podcast, completely absorbed in the ideas—nodding along, having aha moments, feeling like everything is clicking—only to find that days later, you completely forgot to use it when you needed to?

You understood it. You believed it. So why, in the moment you really needed it most, did it feel like you never learned it at all?

I walked into the divorce mediation appointment thinking I was ready.

I had rehearsed every possible scenario, mentally prepared myself for anything that might come up, and committed to staying grounded no matter what.

I knew my truth. I had my tools. I was determined to rise above.

But within minutes, everything unraveled.

The mediator immediately told me the documents my lawyer prepared didn't match what I was telling him. And, of course, as lawyers sometimes have been known to do, he did it with a casual, condescending tone.

And suddenly, I felt it: the shift.

I didn't have control of myself anymore.

I was watching as my voice and words were completely hijacked.

My heart was thundering. My limbs were twitching. And everything inside of me was screaming to get out of this room.

It wasn't just a stress response; it was primal.

I was like a cornered animal—small, shaking, wild-eyed. Two predators closing in, and nowhere to run.

I was unraveling, and I just kept spinning—faster, louder, more erratic.

And the worst part was, I knew it. I knew I was unraveling. I just couldn't stop it.

I was trapped watching as the whole room turned into a wildlife documentary narrated by David Attenborough:

> *"Here we see the female, backed into a corner, eyes wide, adrenaline surging. Her options are limited. Fight or flee. But to do anything other than submit confirms to the predator, she is crazy ..."*

I stood up. I shouted. I paced like something feral.

I talked over them both, trying to reclaim oxygen in a room that suddenly had none.

I wasn't trying to make a scene. I was doing exactly what every prey animal does out of instinct on those nature shows—make yourself appear larger. Buy a few seconds of safety. Fool the threat into thinking maybe you're not worth the chase.

And the more scared I got, the bigger my movements became. Arms flailing. Voice rising. Like if I could just get big enough, just take up enough space, maybe I could scare them off. Maybe I could finally be the threat instead of the prey.

But it didn't work.

Because these predators weren't backing down. One was trying to manipulate me into agreeing to things I didn't agree with. The other was pretending he was a victim.

But this wasn't about John. Or the mediator. Or even the divorce.

This was courtroom trauma. Childhood panic. Years of being trapped in systems where I wasn't safe and couldn't leave. Where no one believed me. Where I had to stay small and quiet and obedient while people with more power made decisions that shaped my life.

And now, it was all happening again.

Same feeling. Same fear. Different room.

Only this time, I didn't stay small. I exploded.

Or at least, that's how it must have looked to them. Like I lost control. Like I went crazy.

The mediator stared at me, stunned. Then said, "Mediation will not be effective for you."

That was it. We were dismissed.

Next stop: Guardian ad Litem. Novalee's fate was in the hands of a stranger.

We walked out of that office like strangers. I don't remember if we spoke.

When I left the building, I collapsed into my car and sobbed. I wasn't angry at him. I wasn't even angry at the mediator.

I was devastated—because I thought I was further along than this.

I had worked so hard to heal, and yet here I was, still not fully free.

That moment pulled back the curtain. It made one thing painfully clear: Transformation doesn't show up in peaceful moments. It shows up under pressure. And in that room, my body told the truth my mind didn't want to admit.

I had understood the lessons. But understanding isn't integration.

What I experienced wasn't a failure of willpower or mindset—it was a textbook example of the amygdala hijack.

When the brain perceives a threat, the amygdala activates the fight, flight, or freeze response. Blood flow is rerouted from the prefrontal cortex—the part of the brain responsible for logic, reasoning, and self-regulation—to the survival centers, shutting down access to the very tools I had just spent months building.

At that moment, my system didn't trust I was safe enough to even try to use them.

That's why trauma work and embodiment practices are essential: Because you can't talk your way out of a survival state. You have to train your body to recognize the difference between danger and discomfort.

I remembered something I had learned early on but hadn't fully experienced until now: the 4 Stages of Knowledge.

Unconscious Incompetence

You don't know what you don't know. There was a time when I had no idea how deeply conditioned my thoughts and behaviors were. I wasn't questioning anything. I was just reacting to life, thinking that was normal. I didn't realize my autopilot *was* a pattern.

Conscious Incompetence

Now, you see the problem—and it's maddening. This is where frustration shows up. You know better, but you can't do better yet.

That's where I was when I started EMF. I could see how I was sabotaging myself, but I couldn't stop it. My awareness was ahead of my ability, and that gap was painful.

Conscious Competence

You can do it—but only if you're paying attention. This was the bulk of my transformation journey.

I had the tools. I knew how to use them. But it took effort. Focus. Intention. The moment I stopped being deliberate, the old patterns crept back in. I could catch myself, but it wasn't automatic yet.

Unconscious Competence

Now, it's who you are. You don't have to think about the skill anymore; you *are* the skill.

The response becomes the default. The rewiring has held. This is true mastery—not perfection, but integration. The moment when doing the right thing no longer feels like effort.

I hadn't regressed. I had just overestimated where I was in the learning process. And even though I could name where I was, that didn't make it any easier when the emotional wave hit.

So, what did I do?

I played "Stronger" by Thunderstorm Artis on repeat. I used the "Grey's version" only because the slight word change between them resonated with me more.

I cried. I sang. I danced through the weight of it. The song moved like I did—slow, deliberate, heavy at times, but always forward.

Put it on now, take a listen.

There is no melody at first—just a beat. Like boots hitting gravel. Like a chain gang breaking stone under the weight of something they never chose.

No flourish. No escape. Just the rhythm of not quitting.

His voice didn't ask me to rise. It didn't cheer or shout or tell me I'd be okay.

It hummed.

It stayed with me in the low place. Matched my breath. Matched my grief. Matched the quiet, aching truth that sometimes healing feels less like flying and more like dragging your feet forward through mud—one strike, one stomp, one step at a time.

That trembling kind of strength that only shows up when you've got nothing left but the choice to keep breathing.

It didn't ask me to be fine. It just asked me to stay.

To stand in the ruin and remember I was still here.

I let it carry my doubt. I let it remind me why I was doing this.

Every time I wanted to quit, that song told me what I needed to hear: You're not starting over. You're starting stronger.

That was all I needed. I hadn't failed. I hadn't broken down because I was weak or incapable. I had broken down because I didn't yet have full access to the version of myself I was becoming.

When you're in survival mode, you don't rise to your level of knowledge, you fall to your level of programming. And unless that programming has been updated on a nervous system level, you will always default to what's most deeply wired.

That's not failure. That's biology.

That moment showed me that this isn't just a personal problem. It's a systemic one.

We give up too soon before we truly have something mastered. We think we've "got it" after one breakthrough, one insight, one experience.

But transformation is not a single moment. It is a process of repetition, reinforcement, and integration until the new way of being is so deeply ingrained that it becomes automatic.

This is the reason why the Life Science Curriculum is structurally built the way it is. And why we teach kids these 4 Steps of Mastery early on.

Students don't just move through each lesson once—they spiral back through it repeatedly, deepening their mastery every time.

Neuroscience tells us that the brain rewires through repetition. Each time a student practices a skill, they're not just learning, they're physically changing their brain's wiring.

True transformation requires more than understanding—it takes structured, repeated engagement because real learning doesn't happen in a straight line.

The curriculum is built with this reality of mastery in mind: that students must experience the knowledge multiple times before it truly integrates. They need to encounter these concepts from different perspectives, through different activities, at different points in their journey.

That way, by the time they graduate, these skills and mindsets are not just things they understand, they are things they embody.

I had been looking at my transformation as an event—something that happens to you, something you achieve, something with a finish line. But it's not.

True mastery is an identity shift. It's when the new way of being is no longer something you practice—it's simply who you are.

That's when the real work began. Not the work of learning, but the work of becoming.

If we don't teach kids this, we're setting them up for the same quit cycles we've all been through.

We celebrate beginners for making progress, but we don't talk enough about what comes next—the messy middle, the moments where they think they've failed, the necessary frustration before mastery.

We need to normalize the illusion of mastery—the false peaks we all hit before realizing there's still more to climb. If kids can understand this earlier, they won't let the frustration beat them. They'll see it for what it is: proof that they're on the right path.

Picture a second grader erasing a math problem for the third time, cheeks hot with effort, and then lighting up when the answer finally clicks.

A fourth grader stumbling over a word repeatedly during a class presentation, taking a deep breath, and continuing with confidence instead of crumbling.

A seventh grader hitting the wall on a science project, wanting to quit—but instead, asking better questions, finding another way, and surprising themselves with what they can do.

A freshman practicing the same chord progression until their fingers ache, only to discover excitedly one day that the music flows effortlessly, as if it's always been there.

Kids who don't see struggle as a stop sign, but as proof they're climbing higher. Kids who trust that frustration is part of the process, not a reason to walk away. Kids who know that mastery doesn't come in a moment, but in the thousand choices to keep going.

Because when they learn these lessons early, they won't waste years thinking they're not good at anything. They'll know the truth: that the messy middle is where strength is forged—and that's how they'll grow into adults who don't just survive challenges but rise because of them.

The One With the Text Message

A story about internal value, abundance mindset, and crying gratefully on the road to Shambala

One of the early modules in EMF was called Money Mastery. It's module 3—right at the beginning—for a very specific reason: Money is most people's top priority.

But when I started writing the Life Science Curriculum, I debated whether to move it to the end. After all, kids don't give the same priority to money that adults do.

They don't fully grasp the real context of money. They aren't stressed about rent or budgeting. Should this really come so early?

Then, I remembered what that module was actually about.

The majority of the work I had to do around money—my beliefs, my blocks, my entire relationship with wealth and worth—didn't start when I got my first paycheck. It started when I was a child.

Before I ever earned a dollar, I had already absorbed dozens of beliefs from the adults around me.

I heard the arguments. The stress. The offhand comments.

I watched how money was talked about, how it shaped relationships, emotions, and decisions.

And I internalized all of it.

This is why what we call "money problems" are usually something deeper. We have scarcity thinking. We have subconscious beliefs about what we deserve and what we believe is even possible.

That's why kids need to learn this early.

Because this isn't a lesson about money. It's a lesson about mindset. About identity. About internal value.

We're laying the foundation before money ever comes into the picture, so kids can build their lives from a place of "enoughness," not lack.

For most of my life, I didn't realize I was operating from scarcity. I thought I was just being realistic.

Responsible. Logical.

But underneath that logic was a belief that there wouldn't be enough—not enough money, time, opportunity, support ... not enough of me.

We didn't have much growing up, but neither did most people around us, so I didn't feel poor. Still, I absorbed this belief.

My dad drilled into us the same broken record over and over again: Work hard, get good grades, get a high-paying job—that's how you'll be happy.

Nothing else mattered.

And while there were moments of what I now recognize as gratitude, they were usually packaged in guilt. "There are starving children in the world, so finish your plate." In other words, be grateful—or else.

As if me overeating would somehow solve the problem.

Gratitude wasn't something I embodied. Abundance wasn't something I'd ever even felt.

That's what scarcity does. It makes you grip harder, chase worth, and measure your value by what you can prove.

As a kid, I thought my value was measured in hours. In grades and work output. How well I could follow instructions.

Someone else always got to decide whether I was worthy—if I got the job, if I kept the job, if I was paid enough to be seen as successful.

I didn't know I was allowed to decide what my value was. I didn't know value could come from within.

And once I did? I stopped asking, "Where can I make the most money?"

And started asking, "Where can I make the most impact?"

I stopped trying to get chosen—and realized I already had been. I already had something to give. Something no one else could do for me or take away from me. Value didn't live in a job title, a paycheck, or someone else's approval.

It lived in my resonance.

In my contribution.

In my being.

The shift started with one thing: gratitude.

Not the performative kind. Not the forced journaling or "be thankful for your shoes" gratitude. I'm talking about the kind that catches in your throat. That cracks you open. That humbles and expands you all at once.

I never understood how someone could cry from gratitude. That didn't make sense to me. Until it did.

It happened with a song: "Thank You" by Alanis Morissette.

You remember her, right? Rage and fire in the '90s—biting lyrics, wild hair, unfiltered pain you could scream along to in a car with the windows down.

Then, she disappeared.

And came back with this ... quiet.

This strange, gentle unraveling of a woman I thought I understood.

When it first came out, I changed the station. I missed the anger. I didn't know what to do with softness yet. I didn't understand where all that fire had gone. I was still an angry teen, burning with my own pain.

But a few months ago, it found me again.

And I bawled.

Because this time, I heard it. It was like the music itself was grateful.

That twinkling keyboard swept through my headset, side to side, until my whole chest felt fizzy and full. Like gratitude, when it's real, it lifts you from the inside.

Grab your earbuds and listen to it.

She's not just singing, she's thanking the hard parts, gently, like an old friend. Not grateful *in spite of* the pain. Grateful *because of it*.

And I finally understood: Gratitude isn't just about what's good. It's about recognizing what grew you. It's about saying, "Thank you for showing me I'm still here."

Gratitude isn't the goal. It's the doorway.

It's the shift that unlocks a new relationship with the world. When you start living in a state of embodied gratitude, you stop seeing life as something you have to fight your way through.

You stop seeing other people as competition.

You stop seeing lack.

You start noticing flow. Support. Alignment.

That's what abundance is. Not having more, but trusting in what you already have.

Gratitude is how we access it. Abundance is how we live it. And the belief in a friendly universe? That's what begins to form when your inner lens changes.

Einstein once said, "The most important decision we make is whether we believe we live in a friendly or hostile universe."

That decision literally shapes everything in your world.

Because when you believe the universe is hostile, you brace. You grind. You armor up. And you repeat what was modeled for you: Chase success, protect yourself, survive.

But when you believe the universe is friendly, you soften. You trust. You move differently. You start to believe that just because someone else has more doesn't mean there's less for you.

That value isn't measured by what you produce—but by what you contribute.

And I had a lot I could contribute.

The moment I shifted into that mindset, life started meeting me there.

I knew I needed to write a book to bring awareness to the Life Science Curriculum. But I didn't know where to start, so I signed up for a webinar hosted by Best Seller Publishing.

Rob Kosberg, the CEO and founder, was walking through his company's success stories—how they help aspiring authors publish and launch their books.

To be honest, I'd been half-listening up to that point—multi-tasking the best I could. It felt like any other business webinar: polished pitches, big promises. I just wanted him to get to the price already. I had a million other things on my to-do list for the day.

But then, Rob casually mentioned *The Drew Barrymore Show*. One of his clients had recently been booked for a segment to discuss her book.

And instantly—like Dug in the movie *Up* when he sees a squirrel—he had my full attention.

Because just days before, I had seen Drew Barrymore on TV for the first time in forever.

I was out running errands, standing at the checkout, when a quiet pull nudged me to look up at the TV—which I almost never do, since it's usually just the "end-of-the-world" news.

But when I looked up, I saw her.

It was like she was talking directly to me. Not literally, of course. But there she was, whole face looking straight through the screen.

"This book is so funny and amazing, and I felt like you were holding my hand through it."

I just stood there, this cheesy smile plastered on my face like "Aww, thank you Drew," as if I was sitting there next to her on the couch. Clearly confusing the cashier standing in front of me, who had no idea where I had just mentally gone.

And as I turned to leave, I said without realizing, "I'm going to be on *The Drew Barrymore Show*! Have a fantastic day!" and walked out.

So when Rob mentioned her, I knew this wasn't random. I wasn't imagining the pull.

I was being guided.

That's when I stopped passively watching the webinar. I opened a new tab and went straight to the Best Seller Publishing website. I didn't want the pitch or the product—I needed to speak with Rob directly.

I didn't rush it.

I poured my soul into that author submission form—my vision for children, my mission, the Life Science Curriculum—my whole heart laid out on the page.

I told him what I was building—for kids, for families, for the future—and why it mattered so damn much.

When I finally hit submit, I whispered to myself, *Talk to you soon, Rob.*

I got the instant auto-response: Thanks for your submission. Someone will reach out within 48 hours …

Probably an intern, I thought. *Someone on the outer edges of the company, reviewing dozens of forms like mine every week.*

Fair enough. So I moved on with my day.

Only, exactly ten minutes later, my phone buzzed. It was a text message from an unknown number: "Hi Sarah. It's Rob Kosberg. Saw your book application."

I blinked.

Of course you did.

"Hi Rob," I typed back, grinning ear to ear. "That was fast."

I knew then that I wasn't just imagining it.

That wasn't just chance. That was truth. That was the universe responding—not to what I said I wanted, but to who I had finally become.

It didn't come because I pushed harder.

It came because I softened, because I trusted.

Because I finally stopped bracing for disappointment and started embodying what it meant to live from abundance. To know exactly what value I have to contribute.

Gratitude opened the door. Wholeness walked me through it. And that belief—that we live in a friendly universe—became not just something I hoped for, but something I experienced.

I put on my headphones and turned on "Shambala" by Three Dog Night.

And I sang and danced like a fool.

Not to manifest. Not to push through something. Just to celebrate.

The song didn't ask anything of me. It just met me where I was—happy, whole, and finally home in myself.

That bouncy rhythm kicked in and suddenly I wasn't in my house anymore. I was on a wide-open road, walking with a kind of pep I hadn't felt in years. Smiling. Waving. People waved back—like they knew me. Like they wanted to join in. Like we were all in on the same secret.

That's what joy feels like when it's real. Just rising up from the inside because something in you finally believes you deserve it.

The lyrics landed with brand-new meaning for me that day. Because that's exactly how life had been showing up. Like it—and everyone I came across—was finally on my side.

Shambala became a symbol for what it means to walk in alignment with your dreams.

Not force. Not hustle. Just flow.

A reminder that when you stop fighting the current, life has a way of carrying you exactly where you're meant to go.

Time to press play.

That road—the one that had been an uphill struggle for so long—suddenly flattened out.

Things flowed. People helped. The right doors opened. The heaviness lifted.

And that's what I want for our kids.

Not to teach them how to chase money, but how to recognize their value. How to trust in a world that reflects it back to them. How to create from abundance, not fear.

Because when they learn this early—when they understand that their mindset shapes their experience—something shifts.

It changes how they show up in the classroom: not afraid to raise their hand, even if they're not sure they're right.

It changes how they walk into a room: not wondering if they belong, but knowing they have something to offer.

It changes how they respond to rejection: seeing it as redirection, not proof that they're not enough.

It changes how they speak up when something doesn't feel right—not because someone gave them permission, but because they trust their inner compass.

It changes how they create, how they lead, how they dream—not to prove themselves, but to express what's already inside them.

It changes their life.

The One With the Glitter Bomb

*A story about emotional loops, event reframing,
and losing my emotional baggage*

Most people think emotions come from what happens to us.
But they don't.

Emotions come from the meaning we give to what happens.

This blew my mind the first time I heard it. Because I had
spent decades believing the opposite—that my emotional state
was something that happened to me. That I was at the mercy
of my feelings. That if I was sad, it was because something sad
had happened. If I was angry, something must have caused it.
If I was hurt, someone had hurt me.

But here's the truth: An event is just an event. It becomes
emotional the moment we assign it meaning.

And that meaning—that judgment—is what starts the loop.

Here's how it works: An event happens. We have a thought
about that event. That thought might sound like: "She disrespected me." Or "I'm such an idiot." Or "No one ever listens
to me."

That thought triggers a chemical response in the body—a
surge of cortisol, adrenaline, sadness, shame, or rage.

We react to that chemical with a behavior—we snap at someone, cry, shut down, lash out, withdraw.

And that behavior often triggers another event.

Event → Thought → Emotion → Behavior → New Event = Loop

The cycle repeats. Over and over. Until we interrupt it.

But here's the thing most people don't know: The chemical surge of an emotion—the actual physiological response in the body—only lasts 60 to 90 seconds.

That's it.

Then, it fades. The body returns to homeostasis. Back to calm. Back to clarity. Back to center.

And then, you kinda let out a little laugh.

I can sense the look on your face right now, and I completely understand and welcome your skepticism. Especially considering how I have been droning on and on now for pages—all woe is me.

But the truth is, those emotions could have ended. But the cycle couldn't stop because we are keeping it from completing.

Every single time.

If we don't add another thought, another judgment, another meaning, the emotion simply runs its course.

But we don't do that, do we?

We think the thought again. We justify it. We replay it. We feed it.

And just like that, we start the loop all over.

That's how I lived for years.

I remember one night—Novalee was maybe three. She spilled a full jar of glitter across the floor right as I finally sat down after what felt like the longest day of my life. I was running on fumes, overstimulated, probably hadn't eaten in hours.

In that moment, my whole body lit up with anger—not because of the glitter, but because of everything behind it.

Every unmet need. Every moment I didn't feel seen. Every story I had ever carried about being disrespected or unappreciated or alone.

My chest got tight. My hands started shaking.

I could feel the words building, sharp and hot, right behind my teeth. But instead of breathing and letting it process through me, I fed it. I kept thinking, *Why can't I have one second of rest? Why is everything so hard? Why does no one help me?*

I snapped. Not full-on yelling—but sharp enough to make her face fall. Sharp enough to feel it in my gut right after.

And that guilt? That became its own secondary loop.

I cleaned up the glitter. I apologized. (Side note: since beginning to teach all of this to Novalee, my apologies are now met with various versions of "Love you, Mom, we're supposed to make mistakes.") But inside, I kept holding onto it for hours. Replaying it. Judging myself. Feeling stuck in a storm I didn't know how to step out of.

That was before I understood what was really happening. Before I knew how to stop feeding the loop.

Before I had a song.

Before I had a breath.

I didn't know I was exacerbating all of this. I thought I was just broken. I thought I had depression. Anger issues. Anxiety. And maybe I did. But underneath all of it, I had a brain that didn't know how to stop.

It wasn't until I started learning about the emotional life cycle—really learning it, not just reading about it—that things began to change.

I started practicing.

When something upsets me, I feel it rise. I name it. I locate it in my body. And I don't think.

I don't tell a story. I don't judge it. I don't assign meaning. I let it be a physical experience. I observe. Nothing more.

And most of the time, it fades.

I return to peace. Sometimes I even find myself laughing.

It's not easy. Especially not at first. But it works. And eventually, the more I practiced, the more I could feel when I was about to loop—and choose not to.

✦ ✦ ✦

But there were times I couldn't stop it on my own. The thought would come in too fast—too loud, too familiar.

Logic wasn't enough to hold me steady. So I turned to music.

Specifically: "Breathe (Slow)" by MC Yogi. It wasn't just the words. It was the rhythm. The tempo gave my nervous system something to anchor to. Instead of counting in my head, I could match my breath to the beat—a full, four-part cycle built right into the song.

Inhale ... two, three, four.

Hold ... two, three, four.

Exhale ... two, three, four.

Hold ... two, three, four.

Repeat.

You can tap your foot or snap your fingers if you need help finding the rhythm. If you're in sync, you'll get through four full rounds before the next part of the song kicks in.

And if you lose your place? No big deal. Just find the beat again and begin again.

That happened to me all the time—usually when I started thinking when I should've just been breathing. Because the moment I was thinking, I was back in the spiral.

I didn't use the song as a distraction. It was more about regulation. It gave me something to *follow* so I didn't have to *fight*. It let me feel the emotion without getting hijacked by thought.

Eventually, I didn't need it as often.

The more I practiced feeling without feeding, the more I could hold steady on my own.

But in the beginning, that song gave me a structure I could lean on. It helped me stay with the storm without spinning back into it.

Put it on and give it a try for yourself.

Once I learned how to stop the loop, I could finally start examining the meanings I had assigned to everything.

The stories I'd told myself for years:

"My childhood ruined me."

"My parents didn't love me enough."

"I have a broken brain, and this is just the way it is."

What if none of that was true? What if those were just meanings I had attached? What if I could choose different ones?

And I did.

Not all at once. Not easily. But over time, I went back through every painful chapter and stripped it down to the facts.

This is what happened.

This is what I learned.

This is how I grew.

I stopped carrying my trauma like a war scar and started seeing it for what it really was: a gift. Not because what happened was okay, but because of what it made possible.

All the trauma I endured—both as a child and as an adult— helped me become who I needed to be.

I didn't get here *in spite of* my past. I got here *because of it*.

And eventually, I could say something I never imagined would be possible: I wouldn't go back and change a thing. That desperate longing I once had to go back and change everything was gone.

Because every single one of those experiences shaped me into the version of me that exists now.

And *she's* the one who can teach this to others. Who can give these tools to Novalee. Who can stand in front of a room full of kids and say, "You are not broken. And here's how to get the chaos to stop."

✦　✦　✦

There's a song that captures this shift more than anything else: "My Silver Lining" by First Aid Kit.

The first time I heard it, I froze.

Not because of the lyrics; those came later. Because of that *violin*.

It doesn't ease in gently. It stretches across the silence with this haunting, cinematic pull—like the opening scene of an old Clint Eastwood Western you know will change you.

It's not sad exactly. It's not sweet. It's *urgent*.

If you haven't listened before, stop here. Put it on. Headphones in, volume up. Let the sound climb up your spine.

Then, come the voices. Harmony so tight it feels like truth. You don't know what they're about to say, but your body already believes it.

And just like that—you remember. That ache inside you? It's just the absence of forward motion.

This song didn't just reflect how I felt. It *commanded* a shift.

I wasn't going to take the easy road anymore. I wasn't going to keep dragging the weight of my story like it proved something. I wasn't going to sit in the waiting room of my own life.

I was going to *find* the silver lining.

Even if it took a lifetime.

Even if it hurt.

Even if I had to let go of everything I used to be.

I let it go. I let myself be free.

And *damn*, did it feel good.

This is why we teach emotional intelligence to kids.

Because imagine a child—let's say a fifth grader—standing in the hallway after a classmate says something cruel.

Their face turns red, their fists clench, and for a moment, the emotion rises like a wave ready to crash.

But instead of lashing out or shutting down, they pause. They take a breath. They feel the anger in their chest, in their hands—and they let it pass. Just like they practiced.

Or picture a middle schooler still hurting from their parents' divorce. They've been carrying around this belief that it was their fault—because of something they said, or something they did. They never talked about it, but the story played on repeat in their mind.

Now, imagine that same student, sitting in a Life Science class, learning that events are neutral until we assign them meaning. That thoughts shape emotions. That they have the power to change the story.

They go home that day and look at an old photo of their parents together. And instead of spiraling, they ask themselves: What if this wasn't my fault? What if this taught me how to be resilient? What if this pain helped me grow?

That's what these tools can do. They interrupt emotional spirals; they help kids reframe the stories they carry and transform guilt into gratitude. Not someday. Now.

They don't have to loop for decades. They don't have to build their identity around pain. They don't have to believe every thought their brain offers them.

We can teach them how to achieve the following: Feel an emotion without feeding it. Recognize that events are neutral. Pause, breathe, and let the body return to calm.

This is not fluff. It's not an extra. It's not a nice-to-have. It's a survival skill.

And if we teach it early, we give kids the ability to navigate conflict without violence. Process pain without collapsing. Bounce back without breaking.

That's what learning how to feel your emotions and process them calmly does.

It hands kids the keys to their own nervous system. Their own mind. Their own power.

Because when you can change your meaning, you can change everything.

And sometimes that silver lining becomes the strongest part of your story.

The One With the Good Feeling

*A story about self-love, judgment,
and getting out of the goop*

For most of my life, I didn't love myself. Not really. Not the way people talk about self-love—the kind that's unconditional, unwavering, and embodied. I loved other people with everything I had. But when it came to me? I was brutal. Hypercritical. Harder on myself than anyone else ever could be. I believed love had to be earned through performance. Perfection. Compliance.

I learned in EMF where that belief begins—with a model of parenting most of us never even think to question.

For the first 18 months of life, most children experience love as completely unconditional. There's no judgment—just presence, protection, and affection. It's the closest thing we have to pure connection.

But around 18 to 24 months, something changes. Children begin to realize there's a back-and-forth to communication. They can say no. Make choices. Assert independence.

And that's often when the "no" starts coming back at them.

No, don't touch that. No, not right now. No, we don't do that.

Parents begin rewarding certain behaviors and withholding attention—or connection—when behavior doesn't align. The child doesn't interpret this as discipline. They experience it as the removal of love—the one thing they've known most consistently until now.

It's not malicious or intentional. But it's nearly universal.

And by the time we form our earliest memories—around age five—we've already been conditioned to believe, *If I behave, I get love. If I don't, I lose it.*

That belief didn't start with me. But it stayed with me for decades. Until I finally found the key to letting it go.

Peter Sage said something that stuck in my head: "You will never rise above your own opinion of yourself." And that line haunted me in the best way.

My opinion of myself was awful. I didn't like anything about me. Not just on the physical side, but also about my personality and my inability to function like a "normal" human being.

Then, Peter gave us the assignment: an Inventory of Awesomeness. List ten things you love about yourself. Add one every day.

It was painstaking. I stared at the page for what felt like forever. But I kept trying. Eventually after quite some time, I managed to scrape up ten generic things I actually did love about myself, like, "I love that I am brave enough to sing karaoke," and "I love that I can always find lost things."

I'd speak the words aloud—whatever I had written down in my Inventory of Awesomeness. Every day. Because repetition creates belief.

I'd hug myself—really hug myself. I tried to look in my own eyes and say, "I love you," but it was too weird. It felt so far away from the truth.

So instead I would say, "I have a good feeling about you. I see all the hard work you're doing. I'm kinda proud of you."

And then, I found the perfect song. Or should I say, it found me.

Find 311's "Good Feeling" and put it on. I heard it in the bathroom while I was getting ready one day. I started singing it in the mirror to myself. It became a daily ritual that bled out into every part of my life.

I sang it in the car and on walks. I listened to it so much, Novalee started singing it all the time too!

It felt silly. And then, it felt good.

And then, somewhere along the way, I realized I wasn't just feeling good about myself anymore; I was starting to love myself. Really love me. And it wasn't a love that disappeared when times got hard. It was pure unconditional love.

Peter once explained it with a metaphor that stuck with me. I'll share it in my own words: Imagine you're down to your last $2. You've got nothing else—no home, no car, just two crumpled bills in your pocket. You're sitting on a park bench, and you take them out in your hand and are staring at them. And suddenly, someone runs by and grabs one.

Just like that—gone.

You'd feel that. Deeply. That loss might break you.

Now, imagine the same moment—but instead of $2, you're carrying two million. Same person runs by. Same one dollar stolen. Same loss occurs. But the impact on you? Completely different.

Now, swap the money for self-love. If you only have $2 of self-love to your name, and someone throws a careless insult your way, it stings. It rattles you. It chips away at the little bit you've got, essentially taking away one of your dollars of self-love.

But if you've built your self-love into millions—overflowing, renewable, ever-present—then, a single offhand comment doesn't even make a dent.

When you hear something like that, it makes sense logically, but to actually experience it is something entirely different.

✦ ✦ ✦

For 18 long months after filing for divorce, John and I were still living under the same roof. It wasn't neutral cohabitation—it was a battlefield.

Some days it felt like he woke up, loaded his verbal ammunition, and fired all day. Digs. Insults. Sarcastic jabs. Little comments designed to land like shrapnel.

He had a way of weaving them into casual conversation, so on the surface, they could be dismissed, but they always had an edge, were always aimed to pierce. It was relentless. Like living in a war zone where the enemy shared your kitchen.

I'd take the hits all day, keeping my face neutral, pretending they didn't land.

But inside, I had a choice to make—either absorb the damage or find a way to make it bounce right off me.

And then, one night after everyone had gone to bed, I put on my headphones and hit play on David Guetta and Sia's "Titanium."

The first beat hit like a pulse through my body. By the time Sia sang the first line, I could feel my whole chest expanding.

Every word was mine.

Every lyric was my truth.

The music wrapped around me like a force field, and something inside me strengthened.

I started moving—first swaying, then dancing—until I was spinning through the living room, barefoot on the hardwood, the lights low, my heart pounding in time with the bass. It wasn't just a song anymore, it was armor.

Every beat was a shield.

Every note welded another layer of protection around me.

And the strange thing was, it wasn't hard, heavy armor; it was light. It was pure, unconditional love for myself, and it made me indestructible.

The next morning, the comments came again. The same old barbs, the same digs, but this time, they didn't land. It was like watching pebbles bounce off a steel wall.

I didn't even need to brace myself. Nothing could touch me anymore.

That's the thing about self-love—real, unconditional self-love. It's not something you put on like a coat, only to take off later.

It becomes part of you. It's armor you carry inside your skin.

But there's a catch. When you start loving yourself deeply, you also start noticing all the ways you've been holding judgment. Not just toward yourself, but toward everyone else. I used to think judgment was harmless—just mental commentary.

But judgment is separation. It's looking at another person and deciding they're wrong, less than, or not enough in some way.

It took me a long time to see that judgment toward others is always just judgment toward myself in disguise.

Every "Ugh, why would they do that?" was really an echo of "Ugh, why would I do that?"

Every time I silently criticized someone else's choices, it was because I hadn't forgiven myself for making my own version of them. And sometimes even because I thought I would be able to choose differently if I were in the same situation (which on multiple occasions has proved to be false when the opportunity actually does present itself).

The truth is, other people's behavior is one of our greatest mirrors.

Every time something irritates us, offends us, or pushes our buttons, it's not just about them—it's a clue about us.

That's why I see triggers as gifts now. They point to the places where we're still carrying old wounds, unprocessed guilt, or a version of ourselves we haven't yet accepted. If someone's arrogance gets under my skin, maybe it's because I'm still ashamed of the times I acted from my ego. If someone's irresponsibility makes me crazy, maybe it's because I still haven't forgiven myself for the times I dropped the ball.

These moments aren't there to shame us, they're invitations.

Every trigger is a spotlight on a growth opportunity, a signpost saying, *Here's a place you can free yourself.*

It's why I love the song "Everyday People" by Sly and the Family Stone. Grab your phone and put it on now. The lyrics remind me that we're all on different paths, wearing different costumes, and acting from different stages of awareness.

Whenever I would catch myself judging someone or even myself, I'd play this song and sing along to remind myself of the truth.

The song makes me feel lighter, like all the stupid rules and divisions we put between each other don't actually matter. It's like Sly Stone grabs me by the shoulders and says, "Stop overcomplicating this—just love people."

Because the real issue here is the complicated rules we attach to love.

We take something infinite, natural, and effortless, and we turn it into a contract.

We turn love into a ledger, with every kindness a deposit and every mistake a withdrawal. We start handing it out like currency—rewarding people when they meet our expectations, withholding it when they don't. We make it a conditional prize: If you follow my rules, you get my love. If you don't, I'll pull it away.

We use it as leverage: *If you loved me, you'd …*

We use it as punishment: *I can't believe you did that. You must not care about me at all.*

We use it as a measuring stick: *Prove you love me by doing X, Y, and Z in exactly this way.*

We turn love into a performance review, as if our worth—or theirs—can be calculated like a quarterly report.

We try to make it perform on command, to fit inside our timelines, to arrive in the exact packaging we think we deserve.

We convince ourselves it's safer that way—predictable, trackable, controlled.

But love doesn't thrive in cages.

The moment you wrap it in rules, you start to strip it of the very thing that makes it love in the first place: its freedom.

When you start seeing people in this uncaged way—through the lens that we're all the same deep down, and we're messy, imperfect, and worthy anyway, the grip of judgment starts to loosen.

You stop treating love like a contract and start letting it be what it's always meant to be: unconditional.

Because the truth is, the more conditions you put on love, the more you shrink it until it's unrecognizable. And the more you remove those conditions, the more space you give for it to grow—wider, deeper, freer.

You can't hold on to judgment at that point, even if you try.

And that's when you're ready to tackle one of the stickiest traps of all: GOOP.

GOOP, as Peter called it, stands for "Good Opinion of Other People."

It's that invisible sludge that gets on you when you care more about how you're seen by others than about being true to yourself. It's what makes you say "yes" when you mean "no." It's what has you editing your personality to fit the room instead of letting yourself just ... be.

When GOOP is running the show, you live in performance mode—constantly scanning for approval, avoiding anything that might spark criticism, and shaping yourself into whatever you think will be most liked.

But when you've built your self-love reserves and loosened your grip on judgment, GOOP can't stick the same way. You start to realize that the people whose approval you're chasing are often just as tangled up in their own GOOP as you used to be.

What other people think of you should be none of your business.

You can't please everyone all the time. People are not going to always respond the way you want and always approve of what you are doing and how you are doing it.

And here's the other thing about GOOP: Once you've washed it off, you finally have the breathing room to set boundaries without feeling like you're doing something wrong.

Boundaries are tricky when you're still stuck in performance mode. You say "yes" when you want to say "no" because you don't want to lose approval. You stay in conversations that drain you because you don't want to seem rude. You keep relationships on life support because you're terrified of being the bad guy.

But boundaries aren't about being "mean" or "selfish." They're about being clear on what's okay for you and what's not—and holding that line with love. Without self-love, boundaries feel like rejection. Without releasing judgment, boundaries feel hypocritical. Without shedding GOOP, boundaries feel impossible.

When those three things are in place—self-love, release of judgment, and being GOOP free—boundaries become natural. They stop being walls and start being gates you control. You're not shutting people out; you're choosing who and what gets to enter your life, and on what terms. And the people who truly love you will respect those gates.

One of my favorite Peter quotes is, "Those that mind, don't matter, and those that matter, don't mind." I recite it to myself often.

Even so, some days I still find myself a little sticky despite my best efforts to avoid the GOOP. I'd start to feel down on myself and right away I'd know to put on "Live Like a Warrior" by Matisyahu.

That's when my shield of titanium turns into a sword. It's not just about standing my ground anymore, it's about moving forward, unafraid, unapologetic.

That song reminds me that my life is mine. My choices are mine. And if someone else doesn't approve, that's their business, not mine. Take a listen now.

The opening guitar grabs your attention—like a call to gather. Then, his voice comes in steady, deliberate, laying out truths you can't help but agree with.

It's like you're at a rally, and he's speaking straight to your soul, reminding you of everything you've forgotten about your own power.

And then, the chorus hits. The energy spills over. It's no longer just a song; it's an uprising inside you. Fierce and unshakable.

A quiet revolution that starts in your chest and ripples outward, where suddenly you remember: *I don't need their approval to live my life.*

Now, imagine if kids grew up with that from the start, before anyone taught them to trade themselves for approval.

Picture a kindergartener who beams with pride over a painting they love, even when their friends say it's weird.

A second grader who laughs off a mistake instead of hiding it.

A fifth grader who raises their hand to share an unpopular opinion—calmly, confidently—because it's true for them.

A kindergartner who walks into graduation knowing they're already enough, without a single gold star to prove it.

A middle schooler who chooses clothes they love, not the ones that will get the most likes.

An eighth grader who shrugs off a rumor instead of spiraling over it.

A freshman who says "no thanks" to participating in gossip and doesn't look back.

A junior who ends a friendship that's been draining them— and sleeps peacefully that night.

Kids who know they're worthy.

Kids who can hold their ground without holding grudges.

Kids who live like warriors—not for anyone else's good opinion, but for their own truth.

The One with Tom and Jerry

*A story about focus, brain training,
and my cartoon criticizer*

Everyone says our attention spans are shrinking.

That we're getting worse and worse at focusing.

That kids today can't sit still for five minutes without losing their minds.

A goldfish has a longer attention span than we do—or so the headlines say.

But here's the truth no one talks about: Our attention spans haven't actually changed that much since the 1800s. The only thing that's changed is how many ways we now have to distract ourselves.

It's not that we've lost the ability.

It's that we've stopped practicing.

Focus fades without practice. Like any muscle, it needs reps.

And full disclosure? I nerd out hard on this stuff.

I mean like "reads neuroscience papers for fun" level of nerd.

I get genuinely giddy when I find out there's a scientific reason for something we've felt all along.

This isn't just "interesting" to me, it's thrilling.

It's like discovering the user manual we were never given.

So yeah, my nerd card isn't just laminated. It's embossed. With gold foil.

We're living in a world that's wired to pull us in the opposite direction.

A world designed to hijack our attention 24/7. Constant dings, scrolls, pop-ups—endless ways to exit whatever moment we're in.

And our kids?

Even if they don't have phones yet, they're not immune.

Walk into a typical playroom, and what do you see?

Toys stacked floor to ceiling.

Stuffed animals, puzzles, books, LEGO sets, dolls, games— more than one child could fully engage with in a month.

Now, ask them to focus on one thing.

How can they, when 29 others are screaming for their attention from the corner of their eye?

We wonder why it feels impossible to sit still, to focus, to follow through.

But after enough practice at being distracted rather than practicing how to be focused—that's exactly what happens.

Now, before we go further—yes, neurodivergence is real. Some brains do work differently than others.

But the bigger truth is this: Even in kids without clinical diagnoses, the muscle of focus has been neglected for generations.

We don't just have an attention deficit. We have a focus training deficit.

And the good news is that muscles can be rebuilt.

Focus can be trained.

For many kids—diagnosed or not—that training changes everything.

And the beautiful thing is, focus isn't just willpower. It's science.

Neuroplasticity means the brain rewires itself based on what you practice most.

There's one specific area of the brain that plays a key role in this process: the anterior mid-cingulate cortex, or aMCC.

Think of the aMCC as your brain's internal grit center. It's the part that lights up when you push through something hard— when you resist the urge to quit, when you breathe instead of react, when you stay with the task even though your body wants to bolt.

Every time you choose to stay, it doesn't just feel empowering, it changes your brain.

The aMCC grows denser and more active the more you use it. It builds more connections. It becomes bigger, stronger, faster, and more reliable. That's neuroplasticity in action. You're not just building character. You're building cortical infrastructure.

This is how resilience is wired—not just as a personality trait, but as a physical structure in the brain. The more often you choose to stay with discomfort—to breathe instead of run, the easier and faster it becomes next time.

And the body helps too.

When we practice things like cross-crawls or breathwork like alternate nostril breathing, we synchronize the left and right hemispheres of the brain, making it easier to stay balanced under pressure.

And focus isn't just about finishing homework or staying on task.

It's also the foundation of connection.

Active listening is one of the most overlooked forms of focus, and one of the most important.

It means staying fully present with another person. Not just hearing their words, but actually listening. Feeling what they're saying. Holding space.

It means resisting the urge to interrupt, to jump in with your own story, or to mentally rehearse your reply while they're still talking.

When a child learns to do that—to stay with another human being in full presence—they're not just training attention. They're building empathy. Emotional intelligence. Trust.

Because a kid listening to a friend tell a story ... and actually hearing them, not just waiting for their turn to talk, isn't just showing focus. They're showing connection.

Quick quiz: What's the body's number one source of energy?

If you said food, you'd be wrong. It's actually oxygen.

And do you know what organ uses the most energy in the body?

The brain. It consumes about 20 percent of the body's total energy.

So what does this mean for us?

It means if we're not breathing properly, we're starving our brain of its primary fuel.

Breath is key. Deep, rhythmic breathing floods the brain with oxygen.

But it's not just about taking any breath. It's about how you breathe.

Our nostrils are purposely mismatched in size, creating a natural vortex that spirals the air as it travels through the nasal passages. This vortex action allows the air to reach the bottom of our lungs, where the majority of our alveoli live—the tiny sacs responsible for oxygen exchange.

When we mouth-breathe or chest-breathe, the air stays shallow. It never reaches those deeper pockets. Less oxygen to the bloodstream means less oxygen to the brain, leading to brain fog, fatigue, and weakened focus.

As if that wasn't enough ...

When you use deep, diaphragmatic breathing, you're also activating your lymphatic pump—the "sewage system" of the body responsible for clearing out toxins. Unlike the circulatory system, the lymphatic system doesn't have a heart to pump it. It relies on breath and muscle movement.

If you're breathing shallowly, you're not fully engaging your lymphatic system. That means more waste buildup, slower healing, and lower energy overall.

Breathing deeply fuels your brain, detoxifies your body, and helps you access your full potential.

Oxygen isn't the only player here though. Hydration is just as critical.

Even just a 2 percent drop in body hydration can cause up to a 20 percent drop in cognitive function.

When you're dehydrated, your brain literally shrinks in volume. Electrical impulses slow down. Reaction time, memory, focus—all of it suffers. And the worst part? You often won't feel thirsty until you're already significantly depleted.

Water keeps you sharp.

It supports focus, memory, and mental energy. It helps carry nutrients to the brain, removes waste products, and keeps all your systems operating smoothly.

Without enough water, it's like trying to run a high-powered machine without enough oil. Things start to grind. Clarity fades. Energy drains.

And no, coffee, soda, energy drinks, and sugary juices don't count.

They might be liquid, but they don't hydrate the brain.

They spike it, crash it, and leave you more dehydrated than before, without you even realizing it.

And even if you're reaching for "water," not all water is created equal.

Tap water meets basic safety standards—but not the standards your brain and cells would choose if they had a vote.

It's often loaded with chlorine, heavy metals, and other residues that your brain and body have to fight through.

Real hydration means clean, filtered water—the kind your cells can actually use.

It's not a luxury. It's the foundation of mental clarity, energy, and focus.

So when we talk about strengthening focus, we're not just talking about mind over matter. We're talking about breath, movement, and hydration—the simple, powerful foundations that most people overlook.

When you fuel your body properly, focus isn't something you have to force. It's something you naturally rise into.

When your body is fueled properly, your brain, heart, and nervous system can finally start communicating the way they were designed to—in rhythm, in harmony, in flow.

But maybe the coolest thing is that your heart has a brain of its own.

Over 40,000 neurons live inside the heart.

And the heart actually sends more messages to the brain than the brain sends to the heart.

When we're calm and breathing well, the heart and brain enter coherence—a powerful, synchronized state where focus, intuition, and energy flow.

When we're stressed? They fall out of sync.

That's why stillness isn't weakness. It's power.

Learning to master your breath, your focus, and your inner state isn't optional if you want to live fully awake.

It's the foundation everything else is built on.

But what happens when the brain and body truly come into sync?

This is wild ...

Your brain literally can't tell the difference between you doing something and you vividly imagining doing it.

There was a study done at the Cleveland Clinic that blew my mind.

One group lifted actual weights. The other group just *imagined* lifting weights—vividly rehearsing every rep in their minds without ever touching a dumbbell.

By the end of the study, both groups got stronger. Even the ones who never lifted a thing.

The researchers found that mental practice alone increased strength by up to 13 percent. The neural pathways fired like the work was real. Because to the brain, it was.

(I'm not saying you can cancel your gym membership and just think your way to six-pack abs ... but the brain's kind of a beast when you train it right.)

Visualization isn't just daydreaming.

It's building the blueprint your brain and body follow.

This is why training focus internally—through imagination, breathing, inner dialogue—is every bit as real as training it externally through tasks and challenges.

Your brain is always building something.

The only question is, Are you building by default, or by design?

✦ ✦ ✦

The real kicker, though? Most distractions don't actually come from the outside at all.

They come from inside of us.

I noticed it so much while writing this book. When the words got hard to get out, or a memory brought up something I didn't want to feel—what did I do?

I reached for my phone.

I didn't even realize I was doing it half the time. It was automatic.

But it wasn't the phone that distracted me.

It was the escape route from the discomfort I didn't want to face.

It's easier to scroll than to stay.

Easier to swipe than to breathe.

Easier to flee than to feel.

Because even if I took the phone out of the picture, I'd just reach for something else instead, like, "Oh look, now seems like the perfect time to clean out my inbox or reorganize my to-do list."

That's the real challenge with focus: not just ignoring the noise, but choosing to stay present when everything inside you wants to run.

This is where the inner battle really begins.

You have two voices inside you: The Criticizer, who tells you it's too hard, you're not enough, you should quit. And the Champion, who reminds you that you're stronger than the feeling. That you can breathe through it. That you can stay.

It reminded me of those old Tom and Jerry cartoons.

You know the ones where whenever they had a dilemma, their inner voices would materialize—the little angel on one shoulder, the devil on the other.

Only in my case, the devil got smart.

He disguised himself as the angel. Kind. Compassionate.

He didn't scream, "Give up!" He whispered, "Be reasonable."

He didn't say "You're not good enough." He said, "Maybe you should wait until you're better prepared."

And just when I thought I was following the right voice ... boom. He'd pull off the mask and laugh.

That's how sneaky old programming can be.

That's how hard it is to tell who's really talking, unless you've trained yourself to spot the patterns.

When I started slipping ... when the Criticizer started getting louder ... I started believing the lies.

The ones that made me feel like I wasn't good enough. That maybe I didn't have what it takes. That I should quit before I embarrass myself.

That's when I'd put on "Sunshine" by Matisyahu. Not to drown it out—to shut it down.

Because the real Champion inside me doesn't whisper doubts. It doesn't shrink or apologize or second-guess.

It stands tall.

It says, *Keep going. Keep your eye on your vision. Don't listen to anything that tells you different.*

The beat drops, and suddenly I've got backup.

Like a bodyguard just showed up beside me, nodding, arms crossed, saying: *She's got this. Step aside.*

It's not just a song. It's a recalibration.

A reminder of who's actually in charge.

Not fear. Not shame. Not that Criticizer's voice in my head.

Me.

So I turn it up, and I walk back into the world with my head high and my feet steady.

Pull up the song. Can you feel your Champion's voice backing you up?

✦   ✦   ✦

This is why kids need this.

Because if you can teach a child that focus is a muscle—not a magic trick, not a personality trait, not "just who they are"—they can change it.

This is what focus looks like in real life: A 10-year-old feeling the frustration of a math problem ... and instead of throwing the pencil, taking a deep breath, resetting, and trying again.

A middle schooler about to pick up their phone during homework ... but pausing, smiling, and choosing to finish the page first.

A teenager taking 30 seconds to do some cross-crawls before a big test ... because they know it will help their brain perform better.

A young athlete visualizing the perfect free throw ... and then, stepping onto the court and making it look effortless.

When kids learn to control their focus, you see it.

You can see it in their eyes. In their breath. In the way they pause, think, and choose.

They move with intention.

And that's how they grow into adults who aren't run by impulse, fear, or distraction—but led by vision, discipline, and heart.

Focus is freedom.

And inner stillness is the doorway.

One breath, one thought, one Champion's voice at a time.

The One With Mayim Bialik

*A story about authenticity, reclaiming,
and finding my people*

When Mikey came back into my life, I knew exactly why.

This was a test. An Earth School challenge.

You say you're a different person now? Prove it.

And I was ready.

I met Mikey when I was 11. Sixth-grade homeroom. We weren't friends; we just happened to share space for most of the year. I think we maybe said ten sentences to each other, total.

Then, in seventh grade, he asked me to be his girlfriend. Huge moment. My first official boyfriend.

It lasted four days.

I honestly don't think we even spoke once during those four days.

On the fourth day, some kids tried to get us to kiss, and I wasn't having it. I walked away, and the next morning found a breakup note in my locker, followed closely by the rumor that he was now dating an eighth grade girl.

The drama!

We didn't speak again until our late twenties, thanks to Facebook. Even then, it wasn't much. A casual hookup situation, not a relationship. That fizzled out fast. And then, we didn't talk again until a couple of years ago.

Once again, Facebook delivered a random message. And once again, I immediately knew what he was after.

He wanted to hook up.

I didn't.

But it turned out we were both going through divorces at the same time. And weirdly, I needed someone who could understand the particular flavor of hell I was in—because they were in it, too.

So I let the conversation continue. And pretty quickly, I decided that he was there for a reason.

This time, he was going to be my practice human. The one I used to practice being *actually* authentic.

Here was my logic: I knew him just enough to feel comfortable, but not so well that I had to pretend or perform. If I acted "different," he wouldn't even notice because he never really knew the old me to begin with.

And as I listened to him talk, I realized something else: He was *John*, kind of. Very different but still eerily the same.

The way he told the story of his divorce—the reasons, the excuses, the righteous indignation—I could practically hear John telling the same story to someone else. The details were different. The pattern was identical.

I told Mikey from the very beginning that we were not going to date. That this wasn't some slow-burn, surprise-love-story twist ending.

Friendship was all I had to offer.

I said it out loud. I said it several times.

He nodded. Agreed. I could tell he didn't believe me, but I moved forward anyway. Because in my mind, I'd done my part. I set my boundaries. I'd spoken the truth.

And so, we kind of became best friends. Well, he became my best friend anyway. We talked almost every day—about the divorces, about our kids, about old classmates and inside jokes from middle and high school.

But this time, I was doing it differently. I wasn't performing. I wasn't people-pleasing. I wasn't walking on eggshells to keep the peace.

I said what I thought. I told him how I felt. If he crossed a line, I didn't shrink—I said something.

I was trying really hard to stay authentic—just be my honest self. I didn't care how I looked because I wasn't trying to date him. I wasn't trying to impress anyone. I was just trying to *be*.

When he started shifting blame or dodging responsibility, I didn't bite my tongue like I used to. I didn't shrink or smooth it over to keep the peace. I called it out. If he did something that rubbed me the wrong way, I didn't internalize it or let it stew—I told him directly: *I don't like when you do that. Please don't do that around me. Or to me. Or at all.*

One time, we had made plans, and the day before, I texted him to confirm. He suddenly started pretending like he had no idea what I was talking about. Being vague. Shady. Kind of a jerk on purpose.

I could feel myself getting frustrated—this old, familiar pull to go quiet and seethe. To shut down and stew in it. But instead, I texted him: "I don't know what you're trying to do right now, but I don't like it. It's making me not want to talk to you or hang out with you."

And just like that, it stopped. He apologized. The game ended. Problem solved.

Then, there was the time we went to the Wisconsin State Fair together.

I showed up as me: side buns, hiking boots with bright orange laces, knee-high purple and orange compression socks, black high-waisted cuffed shorts, and a square-shaped mossy green cropped athletic tank with a sports bra underneath.

Functional. Comfortable. 100 percent authentic.

And the second he saw me, I caught it.

That look.

The *Holy hell, I can't be seen with someone dressed like they just got back from the Swiss Alps with Heidi* look.

I felt his judgment hit me like a bag of bricks. He didn't even have to say anything.

But I didn't care. It was hot. My feet weren't going to scream halfway through the day. I was comfortable. That was enough.

Still, there were moments where I did feel hurt by things he said or did. But instead of spiraling or blaming him, I started asking why.

Why does this hurt?

And most of the time, the answer was simple: Because I was expecting him to be someone he's not. I was holding him to *my* invisible checklist of how "my" best friend Mikey should act—and when he didn't fit, I got upset.

I was trying to force a puzzle piece into a space it didn't belong.

We all do that. We get so caught up in who we *want* people to be, we stop seeing who they actually are.

And though I could see Mikey for exactly who he was most of the time, Mikey couldn't see himself at all. He struggled with authenticity.

He didn't like conflict. He didn't want to upset anyone. He'd contort himself to avoid discomfort. He'd tell me what his goals were—what kind of life he wanted—and then, I'd watch him make decision after decision out of fear ... each one quietly dragging him further from the very life he said he wanted.

And yeah, sometimes I caught myself doing it too. Not just with him. With other people in my life. Trying to shape their perception. Trying to manage how I was *seen*.

Authenticity isn't a one-time decision. It's a lifelong practice. And there are endless opportunities to slip out of it.

Worse are the moments when I catch myself trying to *prove* my authenticity to people who never really saw me in the first place.

That's when I realized: I needed a failsafe. A built-in override. Something that would launch a full-body sequence to snap me back into alignment with who I really am.

I was at Novalee's end-of-year celebration, and the kids were up on stage, singing songs from *Mary Poppins*. So I thought, *Perfect. She's never seen the movie. Let's watch it together.*

We were cuddled up, and we got to the scene with *Supercalifragilisticexpialidocious*—you know the one. Mary's explaining that it's the word you use when you don't know what else to say. When your brain freezes or your tongue ties or the moment's just too big for ordinary language.

And something about that idea stuck with me.

What if I could use *that*—or something like it—as my trigger phrase?

My emergency eject button. The thing that snaps me out of the loop and launches me back into authenticity. But no matter how fun or whimsical it was, that word didn't really do it for me.

It didn't pull me into authenticity … It pulled me into Disney. Still, it got the gears turning. And that's when the *real* trigger dropped in.

Grab your phone. Pull up "Live Your Life" by T.I. And right as you hit play, speak the following words out loud: "Miya hee, miya haa, miya hoo, miya ha-ha."

The launch sequence begins.

Let the phrase repeat. Let it sink in. Let it embed into your subconscious.

The chorus starts.

The beat kicks in.

And something in you shifts.

Your spine straightens.

Your chest lifts.

Your chin finds the horizon again.

And suddenly, you remember who the hell you are.

The nonsense fades. The people-pleasing dissolves. The need for approval, the watered-down words, the overexplaining—gone.

Because authenticity isn't just a concept. It's a frequency. A posture. A vibe—the purest one in fact.

It's the way your cells vibrate when you're finally living in alignment with yourself—your truth, your goals, your dreams, your values, and your weird and wonderful ways of being.

That's what the lesson on Authenticity teaches in the curriculum. It explains to kids that when they can be themselves—*fully* themselves—in every room, with every person, no matter what …That's when they earn their "Certificate of Authenticity."

And in my opinion, that's the only piece of paper worth chasing (sorry Rhianna!)

And once they have it, you can forget about framing it. This one doesn't hang on a wall.

It shines through their eyes. They see it every time they catch their reflection … and you'll be able to see it reflecting there too.

✦ ✦ ✦

I tried to guide Mikey. Tried to get him to loosen his grip on who he thought he *should* be—how others wanted him to act—and just ... be himself.

I think I helped, a little. But you can't force a horse to drink, right? You can only lead them to the water.

At some point, I had to accept the truth: He wasn't ready.

Not to see the world differently.

Not to see himself differently.

And definitely not to see *me* differently.

He was still stuck on the version of me he had in his head. The "me" he wanted to fit into his "happily ever after" piece. And that meant he wouldn't allow himself to be my friend. Not really—not when it mattered. Not when I really needed one.

So a few months ago, I ended the friendship. And I'd be lying if I said it didn't hurt like hell.

I love Mikey. He's a good, kind person. But the truth is, he's not able to meet me where I need a best friend to meet me right now—authentically.

Honestly.

Without the masks, without the fear, without the script.

I couldn't keep waiting around. I had to keep moving forward—to keep following *my* path.

And this ... this is the part they never talk about in self-help books.

How once you finally find who *you* are, you look around and realize—no one else really sees you. No one else is meeting you at that same level of truth.

You've outgrown them.

Not out of ego. Out of necessity.

They don't talk about the grief that comes with that. The hollow weekends. The silent birthdays. The empty feeling you get as you go to tell someone some good news, and you realize there is no one there to share it with. Or you are having the worst day and just need to fall apart on someone, and there is no one.

They don't tell you how painful it is to still find your fingers reaching for your phone out of habit—checking for messages that won't come.

They don't warn you how hard it is to keep choosing yourself when all you want is for someone else to choose you first.

It's lonely.

Because it wasn't just Mikey I had to say goodbye to. It was my family, too. My mom. My dad.

I couldn't be around them. Not by their rules. Not by their fears. Not by their version of what's possible or acceptable or allowed.

I couldn't keep breathing in the shame. Couldn't sit at a table built on blame. Couldn't carry the weight of all the unspoken rules anymore.

The ones about not burdening anyone. The ones about what I was capable of—and what I wasn't. So, I wrote them letters.

To my mom, I told her how I catch myself holding back around her. How I stop myself from sharing my ideas, my plans—because her first response is always to list a hundred reasons why it won't work. I told her how I've noticed that reflex showing up in *me* now, with Novalee—and how I'm fighting like hell to break the cycle.

There was more. Things that were going on for both of us at the time.

She didn't respond well to any of it.

To my dad, I wrote about my brain. About discovering my autism. About finally understanding how I work—how I see the world, how I move through it.

I told him I don't want to live like I used to anymore. Like he still does—bitter, angry, hating my life. Blaming everyone and everything for how it turned out. Treating people like crap because I feel like crap.

He didn't respond at all.

I'm not going to lie—it sucked the air right out of me for a moment.

Like a cross-breeze through an old house—rushing in, stealing all the oxygen, and slamming the door shut behind it.

Boom.

But this is the work.

This is the moment.

The moment I stopped trying to prove myself to people who couldn't see me—and started asking why I keep surrounding myself with people who *never could*.

The moment I stopped wondering if I was too much or not enough—and just decided that I *am*.

The moment my silence stopped being a punishment and became a boundary.

The moment being alone stopped feeling like loneliness and started feeling like clarity.

And then, that *boom* started repeating.

Boom ... Boom ... Boom ... Boom ... almost like footsteps.

Earbuds in. Press play on "Boom" by X Ambassadors.

Feel it.

This isn't a sad moment. It's an *empowering* one.

Let the rhythm pulse through you. Let it move you forward.

Free.

Toward yourself.

✦　✦　✦

I love my parents. I love Mikey. I'm grateful for them. But I couldn't keep staying in a relationship dynamic that chipped away at me. I couldn't share my ideas, my progress, my joy—without them trying to pull me back in. Without them affecting me in ways I didn't always see right away but *always* felt later.

And *that's* why this part is so important.

Because our environment—what we surround ourselves with—doesn't just *influence* us. It *programs* us.

And it's not just who's around you. It's what echoes in your mind after they've gone.

Maybe you've heard of the law of conformity before. Maybe not. But if my science teacher had stood at the front of the classroom and said: "It is a scientifically backed law of the brain that 95 percent of who you become will be determined by your environment and peer group … the people you spend the most time with daily," my head would've snapped up. And I'm pretty sure I wouldn't have been the only one paying attention.

Because that's not just a cute motivational line. It's neuroscience. It's reality.

Your brain is wired to adapt. To belong. To conform.

Not because you're weak—but because that's how humans survive.

Mirror neurons. Pattern entrainment. Nervous system resonance.

We don't get the tribe we *deserve.* We get the tribe that matches our *nervous system.*

If your baseline is guilt and overgiving, you'll attract people who need caretaking. If your baseline is rejection, you'll find people who abandon you early—just to get it over with.

Mirror neurons don't just mimic behavior. They mimic *state.*

Your body learns how to *feel* from the people around it. It calibrates to the room.

It's physics. It's biology.

And if no one teaches you how to choose your environment on purpose ... it will choose *you* by default.

That's why this isn't just about me.

It's about the kids.

Because if we want our children to grow up anchored in self-worth, we have to give them the tools to do what we never had permission to do: To walk away. To say no. To recognize when they are no longer being true to themselves. To know when love becomes manipulation. When connection becomes control. And when "being a good son or daughter" becomes a muzzle that keeps them from breathing.

Yes, it might make some parents uncomfortable. It might create friction, especially with adults who haven't done their own work.

And yes, there will be those who say, "But what if this makes kids stop talking to their parents?"

And the honest answer is: Maybe it will.

You can't send your kid to *alignment school* while you keep worshipping your own chaos.

If we don't grow, if we don't heal, if we keep projecting our wounds onto them—then, yeah, our kids might start drawing boundaries they've learned to set that we're not emotionally equipped to handle.

But that's not a reason to avoid this.

That's the reason to do it.

The kids aren't the threat. They're the mirror. And if we're brave enough to look, they will reflect back everything we need to see, to shift, to finally release.

That's why I created the Parent Companion Path to go alongside the Life Science Curriculum the kids are learning in school—so we don't have to be left behind when our children begin to rise.

So we don't drag them down with us and call it love.

So we don't violate the universal laws of physics and expect their energy to orbit us while we refuse to evolve.

We rise together.

And when they reach that moment—the one where they feel the urge to dim themselves just to be chosen, or stay silent just to keep the peace, or abandon who they are just to be loved—they'll remember: Being alone is not a sign that they're wrong. It's often proof that they are finally vibrating at a level their old cast simply cannot reach.

But they won't really be alone.

Because thanks to Life Science, they'll have classmates and teachers walking the same path. They'll be surrounded by peers who are learning how to think differently, live differently, love differently.

The entire school becomes the ideal environment.

And I know I won't be alone forever either.

I'll find my people. The ones who *get* me. Who *see* me. Who I can be fully, unapologetically authentic around.

I'll find my BFF. The Thelma to my Louise. The Will to my Grace. The Ethel to my Lucy.

Maybe it happens at a science conference. Maybe I look up during a break, lock eyes with Mayim Bialik—and in that moment, "Somebody Sometimes" by Fitz and the Tantrums starts playing in both of our heads simultaneously.

We smile. We dance our way over to each other—because of course, we do.

And when the song ends, we lock arms and head straight to a science lab where she hooks electrodes up to my brain to check out the gamma coherence.

Then, we have some ridiculously delicious vegan food, and we sit and talk about consciousness and cognition and our kids, and we laugh so hard we forget what time is.

What can I say—a girl can dream.

But in the meantime, until my authentic BFF puzzle piece is found, you can put the song on—and be a part of my dancing tribe.

The One With the GPS

A story about goal setting, intuition,
and making wrong turns

What's the craziest dream you've ever had for yourself?

Novalee wants to go into the TV. Not be on it—*in* it. Like Wonkavision from *Willy Wonka*. Full-body transport. Cartoon physics. Zero limits.

Me? I never let myself dream like that. I made goals. Strategic ones. Safe ones. If I didn't know how to make it happen, I didn't let myself want it.

But this time was different.

I had found my gifts. I had found *me*. And I wanted to use the brain I once believed was broken—to change the world. To turn EMF into something kids could actually *use*. Something that helps them now. Not later. *Now.*

That dream was so big it scared me. So big I almost walked away from it more than once.

That's when I play "Daydream" by Lily Meola.

If you've never heard it, stop reading—right now—and go press play.

Let the opening notes wrap around you like a sigh. Let the softness of her voice melt into your chest. Close your eyes. Breathe it in.

This isn't a song that shouts. It doesn't need to.

It's not here to convince you—it's here to *remind* you.

Remind you of the dream you buried under grown-up logic. Remind you what it felt like to believe in something that didn't make sense on paper, but made perfect sense in your soul. Remind you that it's okay if it scares you. It's supposed to.

Every time I hear it, I remember, this dream is mine. It doesn't have to be loud. It just has to be *real*.

And if it still lives in me, then it's not over.

This time, I'm not shelving it.

I don't need to know how it's going to happen. I just need to remember it's mine. And that's enough to start.

In the beginning, I thought my DCA was opening a wellness studio. DCA stands for Definite Chief Aim. As described by Napoleon Hill, it's a small part of your dream you can focus on like a laser beam. He called it a "magnificent obsession."

It made logical sense to me at the time. My dream was the Life Science Curriculum, but I knew I couldn't just walk into schools and expect them to hand over their classrooms. I thought the studio would be the bridge; the way to introduce these tools to the parents first.

It was definitely the scenic route, but I had it all mapped out perfectly.

Unfortunately, no matter how clear it looked on paper, the path wouldn't open. Money wouldn't come. Ideas would fall through. Everything felt heavy, blocked off.

The signs were all around me, literally. The universe, with its impeccable sense of humor, made sure I saw them. Like the sign staring at me the day I stepped out of my car at the dojo next to my chiropractor. In bold, undeniable letters, it read, "No one is coming to save you—best get to work."

I had to laugh. Message received. But even after that realization—after years of knowing in my bones that something had to change with my approach—I still didn't know how it would happen.

Until I did.

It started with a simple text.

The former director of Novalee's school messaged me, asking if I wanted to meet up and talk about ideas for the fall. And then, over a long walk in the forest, she dropped a bomb on me.

One of the other school moms had bought a property.

They—and two other parents—were opening their own school.

At first, I was only thinking about what this meant for Novalee. I was wrapped up in her needs, her education, her future. School was supposed to be the one thing that stayed the same for her.

I completely missed what was right in front of me.

It took almost two weeks for the realization to hit.

I was in the bathroom, getting ready for bed, my mind drifting in that quiet space between thoughts. My binaural beats were playing softly in the background.

And then, lightning.

A thought so powerful it stole the air from my lungs.

I gasped. *This is it. This is the moment I had been waiting for. The moment I had been dreaming about for the last three years.*

This wasn't just another school opening.

This was my chance to get the Life Science Curriculum into a school.

Here's the thing: This moment didn't happen by accident. It wasn't luck. It wasn't coincidence. It was alignment.

Because three years before this, I had no clue how this would happen. I had no school. No connections. No idea how to bring this to life. All I had was a vision.

And I held it.

I focused on who I needed to become to make it real.

And then, the "how" revealed itself.

Like magic. Except it wasn't magic at all. It was a process.

And this moment—the moment I gasped in my bathroom, the moment I realized what had just happened—was proof.

It was the first real-world confirmation that Life Science works. I had followed the exact steps it teaches, and it brought me right to the door I needed.

If the real dream is to bring a curriculum like EMF to kids in every school, then the correct DCA isn't about convincing people to want the curriculum before it's even written—it's about *writing* the curriculum.

Peter's words are engraved in my brain: The rest of the "how" doesn't matter.

And just like that, the resistance disappeared.

And I emailed the school the next day and told them, "I wrote this curriculum, and I want to teach it at your school."

It wasn't actually written. But as Peter says, it's not lying—it's just telling the truth in advance. I did start writing it that day.

Suddenly, it was happening. No longer a theory. No longer a someday idea. This was it.

Letting go of the studio and putting my curriculum on the page was my recalculation.

Because goal setting works a lot like using a GPS.

You start by programming in your final destination—your big goal. You need the exact address. All the details. Because if you don't input a destination, or if it's too vague, the GPS can't help you.

And if the address is slightly off, you'll end up somewhere you didn't mean to be.

Naming my dream of the Life Science Curriculum felt like locking in a destination.

Once the system knows where you're going, it scans everything—the roads, the traffic, the construction zones, the detours—and calculates the most efficient path from where you are now. You don't have to map it yourself. You just follow the prompts.

"Right turn, 1000 feet ahead" might show up in real life as an unexpected email in your inbox about a free webinar on how to use AI to assist with book writing the day after you decide to write a book and meditate on where to begin.

That's the signal. The nudge. The "this way."

From the start though, we question the GPS. We ask, "Why are you taking me that way?"

We don't trust it has a good reason, so we go our own way—and BAM! Traffic jam.

I tried to make my own route by making the DCA opening a studio instead of just trusting the GPS would tell me when I needed to take action and where.

I absolutely still want to open my studio to help others. It's going to happen—just not until the GPS tells me it's time to turn there.

That's goal setting. It's not about controlling the route. It's about locking onto the destination and trusting the system inside you to adapt.

And it will.

You see, the purpose of setting a goal isn't to achieve it—it's to become the version of you who can. It's about stretching yourself outside of your comfort zone to grow and expand into the person worthy of having that goal.

And once you've become that person—in mind, body, and spirit, without needing the goal to prove it—that's when it shows up.

When I shifted my internal state—when I stopped pushing and aligned with the outcome—I wasn't just thinking differently. I was *chemically becoming* the version of me who already had it. That's what triggered the shift.

And that's not just a nice spiritual idea.

It's physics. It's biology. Real science.

Let me show you! (Are you feeling my excitement?!)

There's a universal principle in physics called the drive toward equilibrium—you'll see it behind thermodynamics, electrical flow, brain chemistry, and even ecosystems. It's the idea that all systems seek balance.

Physicists might not call it the "Law of Balance and Harmony," but it's written into the fabric of everything.

Hot things cool down. High pressure disperses. Charged particles neutralize. Your nervous system regulates itself. The weather stabilizes.

Even your emotions follow this arc—rising, cresting, releasing.

So, when you get clear on a vision—and align your thoughts, emotions, and actions with it—you become a new system.

One that's broadcasting, *This is already who I am.*

And the universe—governed by that same principle—can't leave that signal unbalanced. It must rearrange circumstances, people, and opportunities to match what you're already claiming.

You don't attract what you want. You attract what you are.

It's not magic. It's resonance. It's coherence. It's how the universe was designed to work.

Now, tell me you wouldn't have paid more attention in science class if you'd learned how to apply it like this!

We've all experienced it.

You're wandering around Target—no agenda—and suddenly, you find the perfect pair of shoes, a sweater you didn't know you needed, and a candle that smells like your childhood bedroom.

But when you're *actively* looking for something—like a specific pair of pants for a work event?

Nothing. Not one decent option in the entire mall.

That's because when you're trying to find something, your system is broadcasting lack. *I don't have this. I need this.* And the universe—trying to match your frequency—reflects that lack right back to you.

But when you're just browsing, your signal becomes, *I already have everything I need.* And the universe, still following the law, responds with more of that energy.

Abundance. Ease. Alignment.

This isn't just spiritual manifesting. It goes beyond the law of attraction or *The Secret*.

In one study by physicist René Peoc'h, baby chicks were imprinted on a robot mother hen.

The robot's path was powered by a random number generator, meaning its movement should've been completely unpredictable.

But it wasn't.

The emotional bond of the chicks—their focused belief that this *was* their mother—altered the robot's path. Their longing pulled it toward them.

If a group of baby chicks can influence a random system with pure belief?

So can I. So can you. So can our kids.

It makes you wonder, *What else could shift if we stopped forcing and started trusting?*

When I stopped fighting for the studio and started writing the curriculum instead, I was triggering this law. I was aligning with the signal I'd been holding for years.

And the universe responded. Not because I forced it. But because I finally matched what I had already chosen.

But here's the catch: When your dream is big enough—and it should be—it's going to scare you.

It'll feel too far away. Too risky. Too unrealistic.

Even when you've done the mindset work, even when you've visualized the outcome, the fear still seeps in. Not the loud kind that screams, *You can't do this.*

The quieter kind.

This is too big for you. No one's going to listen. What if they don't care? What if this doesn't matter as much as you think it does?

It's the kind of fear that doesn't slam on the brakes. It just starts nudging you off course. A few degrees here, a delay there—until you're circling the same block, wondering what happened.

But I've learned to recognize that feeling now. The slow drift. The subtle disconnect. And that's when I put on "The Greatest" by Sia.

Not in the background. Not for ambiance.

I mean full volume. Headphones in. Lights off. Eyes closed.

Give it a try now.

Because this song doesn't politely cheer you on. It grabs your soul and says, *Move.*

It doesn't ask me to be fearless. It just dares me not to disappear again.

The second that first bass thump hits, something inside me lights up. I can feel the pulse in my ribcage. Like my body remembers before my mind does.

And then, her voice comes in—raw, electric, urgent—and it cuts straight through the noise in my head.

It's a decision. A defiance.

And I dance.

I dance like I'm shedding old skin. Like I'm letting something necessary move through me.

I sing too—loud, off-key, messy. I sing until my lungs burn and my doubts melt.

Because I've left myself behind before. I've tucked dreams away in journals. I've told myself to wait. To be practical. To be small.

But not this time. This time, I'm choosing differently.

And just like a GPS, my system didn't give up on me either. It didn't say, *Sorry, you blew it.* It just quietly recalculated.

That's what this all is: a recalculation.

A reminder that the path might change, but the destination hasn't.

So, I keep going.

Because even when I lose my way, the music remembers.

And deep down, I still know exactly where I'm headed—and that's enough.

This is what I want for our kids.

Not to chase the wrong goals for years before realizing why it never felt right. Not to crumble the first time something doesn't go their way. Not to grow up believing they need permission to want what they really want.

I want them to know how to choose goals that light something up inside—not ones that just check boxes.

To know what it feels like to *want something*—and *not quit* when it gets hard.

To understand the difference between failure and feedback.

To know how to pause, reset, and recalibrate instead of giving up entirely.

A fifth grader learning how to stop before they spiral—because they remember the destination always stays the same even if the route to get there changes.

A middle schooler writing down their DCA and actually feeling excited instead of overwhelmed.

A teenager choosing to set a goal that matters to them—not to their parents, or their coach, or their school—but to *them*.

Because once they learn how to set goals from the inside out, the whole game changes.

They don't just achieve more. They grow into someone who trusts themselves.

And that?

That's a goal worth choosing.

The One With Multiple Personalities

*A story about archetypes, identity,
and getting all my selves on the same page*

Some nights, I was unstoppable.

I'd make a plan. Set my alarm. Lay out my clothes. Hype myself up like I was about to headline a TED Talk.

Tomorrow is the day, I'd think. *We're doing it. We are becoming That Girl.*

And then, the morning would come.

And I'd hit snooze. Twice. Sometimes three times.

And I'd lie there, blinking at the ceiling like, *Wait ... who the hell was I last night?* Because *this* version of me? She wanted none of it.

She wanted sleep ... and maybe an everything bagel with cream cheese.

It was like my entire personality got swapped out while I was unconscious. Like someone came in during the night, pulled the batteries out of Motivated Me, and replaced her with *her cousin*, Lazy Lucy.

At first, I thought I was just inconsistent. Or dramatic. Or allergic to routine.

But eventually, I realized something: I wasn't one person who couldn't get it together.

I was four different people trying to drive the same life.

And no, not in a *Sybil* kind of way. (Though wouldn't that be a wicked plot twist for this book?!)

These were full-blown archetypes. Internal identities.

There's a framework we use in EMF of four core archetypes—or personalities, that live inside all of us. Each one has a unique frequency. A particular flavor of thought, emotion, and behavior. And at any given moment, one of them is leading.

Think of it like this: At some point in your life (or even just in today if you're like me), you have probably embodied the personality and characteristics of a Monica, a Ross, a Rachel, a Phoebe, a Joey, and a Chandler.

They aren't invented characters or myth.

They're part of the human blueprint.

You've met them before. You just didn't know their names.

So please allow me to reintroduce you to, well ... you.

First up we have the Warrior. The Warrior is action. Drive. Execution. It's the checklist dominator, the late-night emailer, the "I'll just do it myself" inner soldier. It gets shit done. Efficiently. Relentlessly.

But leave it in charge too long, and the Warrior burns out—or worse, burns bridges. It starts to confuse productivity with worth. It powers through when it should power down.

Next, the Lover. This is connection, empathy, harmony. It's the part of you that longs for peace, belonging, and to contribute. It's the nurturer, the forgiver, the one who can feel someone's pain before they say a word.

But an unbalanced Lover? They stay quiet to keep the peace. They sacrifice their needs for approval. They disappear into everyone else's expectations—and call it kindness.

On to the Magician. Our head of creativity and vision. The playful one. The intuitive spark. The inner alchemist who connects dots others don't even see. It's your inner world-builder, your brainstorm generator, your midnight idea machine.

But left unchecked? The Magician becomes mischievous. The manipulator. The one who crafts brilliant excuses instead of real action. Who can justify anything to do nothing.

And finally, there's the Sovereign. The Sovereign doesn't yell. Doesn't rush. Doesn't play favorites. But it's the one with the real power—because the Sovereign chooses who gets to drive.

The Sovereign doesn't act from impulse or emotion. It pauses. It listens. It surveys the moment and calmly asks, "Who is needed right now?"

That's the magic.

Not just recognizing your archetypes—but knowing how to consciously choose who takes the wheel and when.

When I first started doing this work, I realized my Warrior was in permanent overdrive.

She was strong—but exhausted. Always fixing. Always doing. Always pushing past her limits like a woman with something to prove.

My Lover? She was barely functioning. Didn't trust anyone. Didn't ask for help. She thought vulnerability meant guaranteed disappointment.

My Magician? Oh, she'd been active for years. Throwing out brilliant ideas at all hours—only for me to procrastinate them into oblivion.

And my Sovereign? She wasn't there ... She was hiding. Tucked somewhere in the back of my consciousness, curled up in a blanket of indecision, avoiding the conflict rising between everyone else.

That's what happens when no one's steering. The energies start fighting. The system destabilizes. And your life starts to feel like a four-way internal cage match with no referee.

Every archetype has both a light side and a shadow side—mature and immature. And without balance:

An immature Warrior becomes cruel. Controlling. Brutal. An immature Lover manipulates with guilt or tears. An immature Magician deceives—sometimes others, often their own self. And an immature Sovereign either vanishes ... or becomes a tyrant.

But mature archetypes? The ones that are fully integrated, awake, and in the light? They become tools. Powerful, beautiful, conscious tools.

The Sovereign doesn't suppress the rest. It doesn't hide from them. It learns to listen to each one with reverence and clarity. And then, it does what true leaders do: It calls them forward, one at a time, and gives them the exact right moment to shine.

Reminds them they're not fighting each other anymore. They're on the same team now. Working toward the same goal.

This is the shift from default to discernment. From chaos to coherence.

And it's not just an internal shift. It changes how you show up in the world. You've seen what happens when people don't know this.

You've seen the Warrior storm through the world with no vision—just force.

The Magician who twists truth instead of transforming it.

The Lover who disappears into silence.

And the Sovereign who never shows up at all.

You see it in leaders. You see it in relationships. You see it in systems and governments and the headlines on your phone.

Because without a balanced Sovereign at the helm, chaos takes over. Power without maturity. Strategy without soul. Brilliance without ethics. Drive without direction.

This isn't about politics. It's about humanity.

Because we don't need more charisma. We don't need more performers. We need more integration.

People who've met every version of themselves—and learned how to lead all of them.

There's a moment almost every day where I have to stop and ask myself, "Who's leading right now?"

Sometimes, when I need to push through resistance and act, even if I'm tired or afraid, I put on Imagine Dragons' "Whatever it Takes."

It's my rally cry for my Warrior. My rhythm for forward motion. Cue it up. Does it get you going, too?

It's how I force myself to sit down and keep writing this book, even when I've walked away from it 27 times so far today.

And when I feel myself about to snap—especially in those parenting or co-parenting moments when my fingers are already halfway through a heated text—that's when I reach for "Dig" by Incubus.

Because the Sovereign doesn't react. She remembers. She leads. She pulls out the best parts of me always. Listen to her song. Can you feel the support and wisdom in her voice?

And when my Lover needs to be heard—when someone I love is hurting, or when I need softness after holding it together too long—I play "Hold On, I'm Comin'" by Sam & Dave.

It's like someone strong and steady is standing at the door, hand on their heart, saying, "I got you." Take a listen. That's the Lover at their best—not weak, not people-pleasing, but rooted. Connected. Willing to show up fully.

And when my Magician needs space to play? It's David Bowie's "Golden Years." Light, funky, creative. Just movement and magic. Play it loud. See if it pulls out your swagger like it does for me.

I didn't choose these songs for my archetypes.

They chose them for me.

They were already playing in my life, each one showing up when its energy was needed.

And now, they're tools. Anchors.

The soundtrack of me becoming the leader I never had.

That's what I want for our kids.

Not to default to the archetype that earned them the most gold stars growing up.

Not to weaponize their strengths or collapse into their wounds.

Not to stay stuck in patterns that don't serve who they're becoming.

Not to be ruled by whichever voice is the loudest.

I want them to know who lives inside them—these parts of themselves.

I want them to practice listening—to feel when their Warrior is tired, when their Magician is spiraling, when their Lover is holding back tears.

And I want them to know they have a choice.

They always have a choice.

Because once you learn how to lead yourself from the inside out—once your Sovereign voice becomes the one you trust—you become whole.

Imagine a classroom where every kid knows these parts of themselves. Where they can name them, hear them, choose between them.

A fifth grader pausing mid-conflict, taking a breath, and saying, "My Warrior wants to yell—but my Sovereign says to wait."

A middle schooler sitting alone at lunch, resisting the urge to shrink into silence—and letting their Lover whisper, "Be kind to yourself. Say hi first."

A teenager reading a cruel text draft, thumbs hovering—then hearing their Sovereign say, "You don't have to win this way."

Once they start asking, "Who do I want to be in charge right now?" they gain the most important skill of all: The power to choose the best version of themselves—on purpose.

That's not self-control. That's self-leadership.

And that?

That's the kind of leadership the future is begging for.

The One With the Airplane

*A story about beliefs, values,
and living like Indiana Jones*

There's a hidden script running your life right now.

You didn't write it. But you feel it.

You feel it when you do something amazing—and still don't let yourself feel proud.

You feel it when you chase goals that don't excite you. When you "do everything right" and still end up in the wrong place.

That's not just bad luck. That's programming.

And if your system was built by fear, shame, or someone else's expectations? You'll keep chasing goals you don't even want—just to feel good for five minutes.

Because beneath every decision, every reaction, every spiral, there's one hidden driver: What do you really believe?

Not what you aspire to believe. Not what you'd say in a journal or a workshop.

But the beliefs that actually shape your day. The ones that decide how you spend your time, how you respond under pressure, what you chase—and what you run from.

Most people never think to ask.

We grow up picking up beliefs and values like sticky seeds on a hike—harmless at first, until we realize we're carrying things that don't even belong to us. Beliefs that weigh us down. That shape how we see the world. That silently run our lives.

And if we're not paying attention, they start running the show.

Here's the first truth we have to face: Our real values aren't what we say, they're what we live.

And sometimes, what we live doesn't match who we want to become.

Values are the compass points of our psychology. They steer us toward what feels right and away from what feels wrong. But if we never question where they came from—or whether they're still serving us—they can lead us in circles. Like the following examples:

The person who values health, but spends hours scrolling, skipping meals, pushing past exhaustion.

The person who values honesty, but avoids hard conversations and sugarcoats the truth.

The person who values love, but withholds it when it's not safe, guaranteed, or returned.

These are loops. Conflicts. Competing values with hidden rules that trap us in fear and frustration.

A loop happens when the *rule* for feeling good actually makes you feel worse. If your rule is, "I only feel proud when I do everything perfectly," the second you fall short, you feel shame instead of motivation.

A conflict happens when two values you care about have *opposing rules*. You want peace, but you also want honesty. And your rules say you can't have both. So you stay stuck.

All your positive emotions are hard or even impossible to earn. All your negative emotions are easy to trigger like a field full of landmines. You're exhausted, resentful, stuck—and you don't even know why.

But here's the good news: Once you see the script—you can rewrite it.

✦ ✦ ✦

I always said I valued adventure.

When I was younger, I wanted to be Indiana Jones. Technically, I still do.

Not like Indiana Jones—actually Indiana Jones. Explorer hat, dusty map, booby traps and all. I was obsessed with the idea of being brave and fearless and searching for lost treasures of the world.

But if someone had looked at my life, they'd never believe that.

I barely left the house. I avoided anything new or uncertain. I talked a big game about adventure—but in practice, I was the furthest thing from it.

Which brings me to the time I flew an airplane.

It was supposed to be a fun birthday experience for Novalee. She'd never been on a plane, and there's a little airport near us that offers short flights for people considering flight school. I figured they would take us up, we'd look around, and come back down.

But apparently, that's not how they do things. We show up, and before I know it, I'm in the cockpit.

The instructor has me start the engine. I steer the plane to the runway—with my feet because strangely, that's how you do it. My toes can barely reach. (This really isn't the ideal setup for the vertically challenged.)

I'm anxious. Out of my element. Trying to listen. Trying to be sure Novalee isn't freaking out or anything.

And then, the instructor turns to me and says, "You wanna take off?"

I laugh. Surely he's joking. He's not joking.

And before I can even think about it, I hear myself say "yes" … Indiana Jones knows how to take off in planes.

He rambles off a bunch of instructions beforehand. I make him repeat them three times. The only one seared into my brain is, "If I say 'hands off,' stop touching everything immediately."

I can't tell if I am comforted or frightened by that statement.

Suddenly I'm accelerating down the runway, pulling back on the yoke, and lifting into the sky. Every cell in my body is screaming *This is too much*. But I'm doing it anyway.

And then, something happens. We level out. The plane steadies. The chaos in my chest starts to settle.

And in my head—I hear it.

"Don't stop me now." Freddie Mercury, belting it out like he's cheering me on from the control tower.

It doesn't feel like a coincidence.

It feels like my body cues the soundtrack the second I slip out of fear and into something else. I don't even know what to call it yet. Just that it's mine. And it's real.

I'm not just watching adventure anymore. I'm living it.

Then, turbulence. The plane bounces. My nervous system goes haywire. My brain queues up every worst-case scenario it's ever rehearsed: *This was a mistake. You're not built for this. Hand the controls back now before something goes wrong.*

I ask the instructor to take over. I stare at the floor. Try to breathe. Tell myself I'm not failing; I'm just resetting.

Novalee, from the backseat, chimes in with, "Mom, I'm bored," and asks if she can watch something on my phone. I laugh. Of course she's unfazed.

But the music's still playing. Louder now. "I'm a rocket ship on my way to Mars" … Like Freddie's refusing to let me off the ride.

I always thought fear was a stop sign. That if I didn't feel ready, I wasn't supposed to go. And so, I never went anywhere.

I close my eyes.

This is what you wanted, I tell myself. *This is who you said you wanted to be.*

So I take the controls back. And this time, I don't let go. We do steep 45-degree turns. I don't feel fearless, but I stay. I focus. I finish the tasks.

And then, the instructor has me land the plane with him. He's counting down as I'm pushing the yolk in 3 ... 2 ... 1 ... and we touch down. He finally says, "Hands off."

I'm shaking. Grinning. Heart pounding. I can't stop smiling. Because that flight didn't just take me into the sky. It took me out of the rules I'd been living by my whole life.

After that, I went back and rewrote my internal code.

Peace became: "I feel peace when I return to my breath."

Success became: "I feel successful when I keep showing up."

Joy became: "I feel joy every time I allow myself to be fully present."

And fear shrank smaller and smaller.

I changed the rules of the game.

And then, I realized ... hey, I really like this game.

I didn't just think differently; I felt differently. I moved differently. I made choices that finally felt good instead of just safe or correct.

This is how we reprogram the system.

Not by forcing positivity. Not by repeating affirmations that don't feel real.

But by rewriting the structure of how we process reality. Because here's the truth: If your system punishes you for joy, you'll sabotage anything that feels too good.

If your rules make worthiness conditional, you'll never stop proving.

If you believe safety comes from control, you'll never trust the flow.

And if you change that?

You stop living on autopilot.

You start living on purpose.

What I want for our kids is for them to learn early that the voice in their head isn't always their own.

That just because they believe something doesn't mean it's true.

That values can be inherited—or chosen.

I want them to catch the moment they start to say, "I'm not brave," and remember that bravery isn't the absence of fear—it's choosing to keep going anyway.

I want them to question the rules running their inner world.

"I'm only smart if I get straight As."

"I can only feel proud when someone else says I did a good job."

"I have to be perfect to be loved."

These aren't just beliefs. They're limits.

They shape every choice, every emotion, every opportunity a child sees—or doesn't see.

But if we teach kids how to identify their values, how to rewrite the rules that define them, and how to build belief systems that serve their growth, we give them power no grade, test score, or reward system ever could.

A fifth grader learning they don't have to earn joy—it's theirs, now.

A middle schooler realizing their worth doesn't disappear when they make a mistake.

A teenager choosing their own path—not to rebel, but to align.

That's how you raise a generation that doesn't crumble under pressure. That doesn't define themselves by performance. That doesn't inherit pain disguised as tradition.

You raise a generation that knows who they are—and who they're becoming.

And maybe they'll never fly a plane. But they'll learn how to fly their own life.

They won't need permission to take the controls because when your values are aligned and your rules make joy easy, you become momentum itself.

And nothing—not fear, not failure, not the past—can slow you down.

The One With the For Sale Sign

A story about higher consciousness, surrender,
and the decision not to chase

I remember standing in the kitchen when my mom said it again: "You're being foolish. Just call the first people back. You're going to lose the sale."

She wasn't yelling. She didn't have to. Her voice carried that familiar tone—disbelief dressed up as concern, urgency pretending to be logic. It was the tone I'd heard my entire life.

The one that said, *You're messing it up. Just do it the normal way. Be reasonable.*

I shook my head. Calm. Certain. "I'm not going to force it," I said.

"This is my life. I don't do things that way anymore." To which she replied: "And look at how all your other ideas worked out so far."

And that was it. It was on.

Like Jon Bon Jovi ... in a "Blaze of Glory."

Blast it now. Loud.

Because the second she said it, every unresolved parent-child moment in human history seemed to burst into a full-blown chorus of that song in my head. And not the polite version.

The primal, shout-it-into-the-wind, fist-in-the-air version.

I didn't even cue it up. It just started playing, loud and unapologetic. A rebel anthem rising from the ashes of every time I'd stayed small to fit into her limited vision of me.

Go ahead: Picture the look on your parents' faces when you tried to be bigger. The disbelief. The eye rolls. The passive-aggressive sighs. Every time you were told to tone it down, play it safe, be more *reasonable*.

Let the words and the music rip through your ribcage.

Let it blast through the silence you once obeyed. Let it become the soundtrack to your refusal.

That's what it was for me: a declaration. A full-bodied *no more*.

My mom didn't get it. Most people don't.

And honestly? Neither would the version of me from a few years earlier.

Because *that* version of me would have panicked. She would have over-explained. She would've called, bargained, rationalized, spiraled. She would've chased peace by betraying herself. She would've mistaken anxiety for action, and urgency for wisdom. She would've thought doing more was the answer—and when that didn't work, she would've done even more.

But this version?

She was done.

Done performing. Done proving. Done contorting herself to meet everyone else's expectations.

I wasn't waiting anymore. I was listening. I wasn't hoping. I was knowing.

And that was the shift I needed.

I hadn't just changed how I was selling a house. I had changed how I was living my life. For the first time, it wasn't about doing what was "smart" or "safe" or "impressive."

It was about doing what was *true*.

Even if nobody else saw it yet.

I was done following rules that weren't written for people like me. And in that moment—standing in her dining room, relaxed, boundaries intact—I realized I was finally living ... the Young Guns way.

✦　✦　✦

I loved that house.

It was probably the hundredth one I'd seen—but the second I pulled up, I knew. Not with logic. With something deeper.

I didn't choose it. It chose me.

During the divorce, I fought like hell to hold on to it. I offered to walk away from other things, to let him have the maintenance, the retirement, whatever he wanted, just let me keep the house. But the longer it dragged on, the more I could feel the truth tightening around me.

I wasn't going to be able to stay.

So I made a decision. If I had to let it go, I was going to use the money to fund my next chapter. Fuel the dream. Burn the bridge behind me. At the time, I thought that dream was opening a mind-body wellness studio. Wrong dream, as you already know, but I hadn't figured that out yet.

What I *had* figured out was this: I wasn't handing the process over to anyone else.

I'd already decided I was going to sell the house myself.

Not just to save the commission, though that was a bonus.

I did it because I knew I could. I trusted my brain. Not because it was trained for real estate, but because it was built for patterns. It's one of my brain superpowers. I don't just notice things, I absorb them.

My brain is like a hyper-speed data-analyzing machine disguised as a tired single mom in yoga pants, juggling snacks and court papers while simultaneously running algorithms on human behavior and the local housing market.

While most people scroll Facebook and forget what they saw five seconds later, I can still picture the granite countertops in a listing from three months ago ... and remember exactly how many days it sat unsold before the price dropped.

And I don't do this on purpose. It just happens.

Real estate wasn't something I studied. It was something I absorbed. The same way I've always *absorbed* people, energy, and truth no one else wants to say out loud.

House listings were everywhere. Dripping through daily life in quiet, uninvited ways: In the background of your scroll. On the town event page where you go to check trick-or-treat times and somehow end up learning that Janet from the PTA is selling her three-bed split-level. I'd see the photos. Note the flooring. Clock the price per square foot. Then, move on.

Except my brain didn't move on. It analyzed and calculated and forecasted all the data without me even realizing it and filed everything away. Somewhere in the back of my mind is a giant invisible spreadsheet labeled, "Real Estate: Probably Useless, But You Never Know."

That's where it went. All of it.

Years of listings. Offers. Upgrades. Paint choices. Lot shapes. Bidding wars. Random facts. All silently filed, cross-referenced, sorted by vibe.

And when it came time to list my own house, that mental file swung open like a vault. And so I knew.

I knew my neighborhood was different.

The prices were consistently higher than surrounding areas. I knew ranch homes like mine were rare, and everyone seemed to want them. Especially families downsizing, or aging parents who couldn't handle stairs.

But I also knew the market was wild. It was spring 2024, and everything felt like a game of musical chairs. Prices were going up, but they weren't stable. It was jagged. Erratic. A glitchy heartbeat. I was admittedly having a hard time spotting true patterns.

So I did what any scientist would do. I ran an experiment.

First, I got a professional appraisal. It came in at $390,000 with a recommendation to list 10–15 percent higher based on layout, upgrades, and condition.

I had the data. New furnace. New A/C. New insulation. New appliances. Fifteen percent made sense. So I went for it: $449,000.

But I didn't stop there.

I ran a second test—this one more subtle. No numbers. No pressure. Just a little bait in the water.

I posted in the subdivision's Facebook group:

> *"I'm going to be listing my home for sale soon and I'm looking for someone to come and give it a clean beforehand. Any recommendations for a cleaning company that can get out here quickly? It's a ranch home, 3bd 2.5 bath. TIA."*

And then, I waited.

Not for a cleaning service. For the truth to reveal itself.

Within minutes, I had a dozen responses. Only one was about cleaning. The rest? "How much are you listing it for?" "Can I come see it?" "We've been looking for a ranch in that neighborhood—are you using a realtor?"

And that was it. Data confirmed. The market was still alive. The house was in demand. And the useless data stored in my brain proved not so useless.

$$\blacklozenge \quad \blacklozenge \quad \blacklozenge$$

The plan was to list by summer. But summer came and went—and so did the hot market.

John refused to sell.

It took months. Court filings. An official order just to move forward.

By the time the green light came, the market had shifted. Prices were dropping. Ten grand here, ten grand there. One blink and the comps fell again. What once felt like momentum now felt like erosion.

That $449,000 number? It didn't hold anymore.

It wasn't just about market value; it didn't feel *true*. And that's how I knew it had to change.

$429,000. That number landed in my body like a tuning fork. Clear. Aligned. Solid.

And I trusted it. So I listed the house For Sale by Owner—as-is. No realtor. No open house. No fanfare. Just three surgical strikes on social media.

That same day, two buyers messaged me. One was a retired couple from the neighborhood, looking to downsize into a ranch. The other, a young couple with a realtor attached.

I showed them both the house. They both came back the next day, this time with family in tow. That's always how you know.

The realtor couple submitted an offer, but it was low. I told them we would be passing unless they wanted to come back with a stronger offer. They declined.

The older couple? They said a cash offer was coming. Said it was just a matter of days. But the days passed. And the offer never came.

A week. Then, two. Silence.

That's when my mom started in. "Just call the first people back. Take their offer. You're going to lose the sale. You're wasting time."

Her voice wasn't just hers. It echoed every parent, every elder, every person who ever told me that survival only came through sacrifice. Who believed urgency equals wisdom. And fear equals love.

I didn't want to react from ego. So I gave myself space.

But I did list the house on the MLS for a small fee to widen the net.

And I'll also admit that her panic wormed its way into my head a little. That's the thing about old programming—it doesn't die when you outgrow it. It just gets quieter, more manipulative.

It waits for a weak moment to resurface. And right before the MLS went live, I caved, just a little.

I messaged the first buyers. Let them know the house was going on the MLS, and they could still make another offer if they wanted.

They replied immediately: They had already put an offer on something else.

And I laughed. Not because I was bitter, but because I *knew.*

I knew right then that my instincts had been right all along. That veering off course wasn't necessary. That the moment I left alignment, the door shut.

So I got back on track.

That week brought more showings. More messages. Still, no offers.

My mom kept pushing. "Are you following up? Are you reaching out? Are you even *doing any of the things I'm suggesting*?"

I wasn't. Because I'd already done the work that mattered.

She called me silly. Said I was wasting time making my "Resource Binder" of homeowner manuals and information. (Which, for the record, *everyone* raved about.)

But I wasn't waiting. I was listening. Not for a buyer. For a *click*. A signal. The moment I would know when to strike.

She was mad that I wasn't doing things her way. Mad I wasn't rushing, panicking, scrambling for control.

But that's not how I do things anymore.

"I don't force it," I told her. "I trust that the right buyer will come at the right time. And I'll get what I asked for."

I meant it 100 percent.

There was no wobble. No inner war between "trust" and "terror." No backdoor obsession with what-ifs.

I was still. And I was *certain*. As if the sale had already happened, and the rest was just lag time.

And just a few days later, an offer came in. It wasn't low like the first. But it wasn't the "right" number either.

By this time, John had changed his tune. Now, *he* wanted it sold. The divorce was final, and he had new financial responsibilities to pay.

"Take the offer," he said. But I didn't even hesitate. That wasn't the number. Our house didn't sell for that.

I countered: $429,000. Full ask. They said yes.

I could've asked for more. I could've squeezed another five or ten grand out of them. But I didn't *need* more. That number was never about strategy. It was about alignment.

And when you're aligned—truly aligned—you don't need to force. You don't need to manipulate.

You just have to choose. And then, hold.

I didn't manifest that outcome with a vision board or spiritual glitter. I didn't hustle my nervous system into burnout to "earn it." And I *definitely* didn't sit back pretending to trust while secretly spiraling about money.

I wasn't pretending. I wasn't posturing. I was *anchored*.

Alignment isn't passive. It's not detachment. It's not sitting in a yoga pose humming abundance mantras while your life burns down around you.

It's fierce. It's active. It's a deep inner recalibration that says: I don't *need* to grip this because it's already mine.

I did the work. Just not the kind they were watching for.

Because the real work wasn't selling the house. It was unhooking from the part of me that still thought she had to *earn* it through effort. That if she didn't push and force it, she didn't deserve it.

This was never just about a house.

This was about the lens I chose to live my life through. Every decision. Every day. Every moment is a chance to choose that lens again.

There are four lenses, actually. The 4 Levels of Consciousness. They're not just mindset shifts. They're *operating systems*. And the lens you're living from changes everything—your decisions, your emotions, your outcomes, your energy.

Here's how they work:

TO ME: The default setting. Also known as *Victim Mode*. Life happens *to* you here. You're at the mercy of your circumstances, stuck in a loop of reaction and blame. You're powerless, even when you think you're not. Sometimes the finger points outward—"They hurt me. They ruined it." Sometimes it turns inward—"It's my fault. I always screw things up." Either way, the question underneath everything is the same: "Why is this happening *to* me?"

I lived there for years. Decades, really. Even when I was functioning—smiling, succeeding, pretending to be fine—I was still stuck in *To Me*. Still waiting for someone or something to save me from the weight of my own life.

BY ME: This is the grind. The hustle. The self-help productivity gospel with a sprinkle of control issues. If *To Me* is helpless, *By Me* is hyper-capable. It sounds like empowerment, and sometimes it is. But it's also exhausting. "If it's meant to be, it's up to me." So you do everything. You plan. You fix. You outsmart. You optimize. You try to outrun chaos by micromanaging every variable.

That's where I thought I was when I listed the house. And to be fair, I *was*. The strategy, the analysis, the posts, the pricing ... it all came from *By Me*. And it worked—to a point.

But *By Me* has a ceiling. It's made of logic and effort and spreadsheets. It's a powerful place to start. But it can't carry you across the finish line.

Because sometimes, power isn't force. Sometimes, it's surrender.

THROUGH ME: This is where everything changes. This is not passive. This is not spiritual bypassing. This is *power*—clean, anchored, unstoppable power. Not because you're controlling the outcome ... but because you've *become a match* for it.

Through Me is when the goal doesn't come from ego—it comes from soul. You don't chase what you think you're supposed to want. You get clear on what's real. And when you move, you move clean.

No spiraling. No proving. No begging the universe for scraps of validation.

You take aligned action—and *release the grip*. You trust the nudge. You hold the vision. And you know it's already done. Even when nothing outside you has changed yet.

That's where I was by the end of the house sale. And that's why it worked.

AS ME: This one's rare. I've only tasted it in flashes. But I know it's real.

It's the moment when the veil drops. When there is no distance between you and what you want—because there is no *want*. You are it.

You're not trusting the process. You *are* the process. You're not hoping for peace. You *embody* it. There's no effort. No longing. No mental chatter. Just presence. Just being. Just truth.

I don't live there. Not yet. But I've been there. And every time I visit, I remember: That's where we're headed. That's who we are underneath all the noise.

The more I learned about the levels of consciousness, the more I started seeing them everywhere.

Not like labels. Not like some spiritual caste system used to rank who's more "evolved."

It's not about judgment. It's about *frequency*.

Some days I'm steady at a higher level. Other days, I drop like a rock. I can be in *Through Me* about this book—clear, sovereign, grounded—and still be spinning in *To Me* terror over parenting.

Sometimes I float for weeks. Sometimes I snap back down in five seconds flat because one stray thought slipped through the gate.

And sometimes? I'm operating in *two* levels at once— different channels playing in different areas of my life.

That's the thing people miss.

This isn't about climbing to the top of some enlightenment pyramid. This is about *knowing where you're operating from—*and why that matters.

Because your level of consciousness doesn't just shape how you *feel.*

It shapes what you can *see.*

It controls what options show up on your screen—what choices you recognize as possible.

And when your nervous system is flooded, when your ego grabs the wheel? You don't default to your highest level. You default to the one you've *trained in the most.*

The one that feels like home—even if it's chaos.

So let's make this more real: Think of it like a video game.

When you first boot up a new game, your character is a newbie. Inexperienced. Under-equipped. Clumsy with the controls.

You don't start out with infinite tools and invincibility. You start out with *barely enough.*

Just like in *The Legend of Zelda: Ocarina of Time.* At the begin-ning, you're Link—just a kid in the Kokiri Forest. No sword. No shield. No rupees. No clue.

But the game gives you what you *can* handle. A wooden shield. A dinky little Kokiri sword. Deku sticks. Deku nuts.

That's it.

And you don't question it. You just use what you've got. You swing sticks and dodge spiders and figure it out as you go.

That's *To-Me* consciousness.

You make the best decisions you can with the tools you currently have. And you don't even know what else might be possible yet. Because you haven't *earned* access to anything else.

But life—just like Zelda—is designed to grow you.

This is Earth School. And Earth School also gives you its version of dungeons. Puzzles. Boss fights. Every challenge you face is designed to teach you how to use what you've got.

Sometimes you clear the level on your first try. Sometimes you fail. Again and again. You slam into the same wall, lose all your hearts, respawn, and try again.

Just like *The Water Temple*. You know the one.

Lake Hylia. Adult Link. The most infamously frustrating, reset-worthy level in Zelda history. People rage-quit that dungeon. They wander in circles. They scream. They Google. They start over. And then, finally, one day, they *solve it*.

And when they do? They're rewarded with the *Longshot*. An upgrade that doubles the reach of your Hookshot. Suddenly, all those unreachable cliffs, hidden doors, and secret zones?

Now, they're accessible.

Not because the game changed. Because *you did*. Because you passed the test. You leveled up. You unlocked new capacity.

And that's exactly what it feels like when you shift into a higher level of consciousness. The world around you may look the same—but you see it differently. You interact with it differently. You have new tools.

New reach.

New access.

It doesn't mean you're done. It just means you've expanded.

But here's the thing about leveling up: Even when you've got the *Longshot*—even when you've unlocked the map and doubled your reach—you still find yourself back in places you thought you'd outgrown.

Not because you're broken. Because that's how mastery works.

You return with new tools, new perspective, new strength.

And what used to shake you? Now, it just sharpens you.

Because this time, you're not bracing for the boss fight. You already know where the traps are. You already know who you are.

You've been here before. But *you're not the same.*

This is where humility kicks in.

Not the performative kind. Not the "I'm so evolved" spiritual ego kind. Real humility—the kind that changes you from the inside out.

The kind that makes you stop mid-sentence, mid-judgment, mid-story you've told a hundred times—and ask yourself, *What if they were doing the best they could ... with what they had ... at the level they were at?*

Because once you start to see life through levels of consciousness, it's not personal anymore.

It's not that my mom didn't love me. It's that she was drowning in survival mode—fighting battles I couldn't see—and no one ever taught her how to regulate her own nervous system, let alone guide mine.

It's not that my dad was heartless. It's that he equated vulnerability with weakness because someone once shamed it out of him.

It's not that John was evil. It's that he was navigating his own unhealed wounds with a limited emotional vocabulary and a map drawn by pain.

And Mikey? He was me, just a few years ago. Trying to make sense of the chaos, chasing healing without instructions. He wasn't the villain in my story. He was the rearview mirror. The rumble strip. The reminder that if I didn't center myself, I could veer off course and end up right back at the beginning.

I'm grateful for every one of them.

Truly.

I love them. I appreciate them. Because each of them gave me something.

Each helped me calibrate. Each gave me a mirror. Each asked the question:

Is this who you still want to be?

And I hope I did the same for them.

I hope I've been a North Star sometimes. But I know I've also been a red flag. A caution sign. A "don't be like her" moment in someone else's story.

Maybe even in yours.

And that's okay. We're all either a warning or an example— often both, sometimes even in the same day.

And I'm grateful I've been both. Because being only one would mean I wasn't growing.

There's no room for ego when you see life this way. No need to compare timelines or count scars. No need to feel better than anyone.

Just ... clear.

Clear enough to forgive.

Not because what happened was okay. But because now, you understand *why* it happened.

You start to see the difference between a person and their behavior. Between intention and impact. Between what someone *thinks* they're doing—and what they're actually doing.

And when you really feel that—not when you just say the words, but feel them in your body? That's the moment you exhale the breath you didn't know you were holding.

That's when "Freedom for a Change" by Gizmo Varillas becomes more than background music. It becomes a shift. A moment. A release.

The apology you stop waiting for.

The resentment you no longer need.

The moment you choose peace over being right.

Take a listen now. The guitar riff rolls in—clean, percussive, unforced. It doesn't demand anything from you. It just opens a door. Simple. Grounding. Liberating.

It lets you set down what you've been carrying.

I've forgiven people who still refuse to see me. Forgiven those stuck in patterns they can't yet recognize. People trapped in survival. People walking through levels I've already passed.

Because I don't need them to change for me to be free.

They are not their behavior. They're not broken. They're not behind. They're just students in Earth School, like the rest of us. Leveling up in their own time, in their own way. And I'm still a student too.

Still calibrating. Still veering. Still catching myself when I drift.

But now? I feel the rumble strips sooner. I forgive faster. I come home faster.

And maybe that's the point.

To remember that Link didn't earn the ability to move between child and adult by escaping the timeline. He earned it by returning. To the Temple of Time. By placing the Master Sword down. By picking it back up again.

It wasn't regression. It was sacred.

Because some puzzles can only be solved with childlike faith.

And some battles require the strength and strategy of adulthood.

And some days you need both.

So the next time someone's acting like a total jackass—before you grab your own sword and start swinging—try this instead:

Picture them as Link.

Tunic askew. Shield missing. Lost in some temple you've already passed. Maybe they just got knocked back a few levels. Maybe they're still trying to read the damn map. Maybe they don't even know there is one.

They're not your villain. They're just another player in Earth School. Still on their quest.

So take a breath. And let them "Ramble On" by Led Zeppelin.

Put on the song now. Listen to their story—their trials and tribulations, and their struggle to find Zelda. Hold compassion for them in your heart as you remember your own quest, your own struggles to find her. And send them love to carry them forward on their journey.

Because maybe—just maybe—you're the mirror that helps them find the next key.

I think about how different my life might've been if I had learned this earlier.

Not just how to be kind. Not just how to "make good choices." But how to recognize where those choices were coming from.

To notice when fear was driving. To feel when I was trying to prove instead of align. To pause and ask, *Am I reacting, or responding?*

And maybe most importantly, to know that none of it meant I was broken. It just meant I was human. A player mid-level. A student mid-lesson. A soul mid-shift.

That's why this lesson exists in the curriculum.

Because kids are already moving through these levels of consciousness every single day—at school, at home, in their friendships, in their hearts.

They're already navigating judgment, ego, resistance, and intuition. They just don't have the language yet. They don't know there's a map. But we can give them that.

We can teach them how to feel the difference between force and flow. How to recognize when they've dropped into fear—and how to rise back into clarity.

We can show them how to choose alignment again and again, without shame when they fall out of it. Because they *will* fall out of it. That's not failure. That's the game.

And if we do this right—if we make this the standard, not the exception—they won't grow up thinking power means control. They won't confuse being right with being wise. They won't waste decades chasing the wrong goal just to feel safe, or seen, or loved.

They'll still stumble. They'll still get triggered. They'll still question themselves sometimes. But they'll know how to come back.

They'll know how to check the level they're playing from. How to listen for the rumble strips. How to return to alignment—not because they were told to, but because it feels like home.

That's what this lesson gives them: not perfection. Navigation. Not rules to memorize. But an inner compass they'll never outgrow.

And the earlier we teach it, the more naturally they'll live it. The more easily they'll trust it. The more freely they'll become who they already are.

And maybe, one day, when their kids are learning it in school too, they'll realize just how far they've come.

And how different everything could have been ... if they hadn't.

But they did.

And that changed everything.

The One With the Movie Poster

A story about rewriting the script, forgiving the old scenes,
and making this life my favorite film

Do you love your life?

Like really, truly love it?

Do you go to bed at night with tears in your eyes because you're so grateful that *this* is the life you get to live?

Do you wake up with electricity in your chest because you can't wait to experience it again?

Right now, for me, the answer is 100 percent yes.

But for more than 30 years, I couldn't even imagine that feeling. For over three decades, I hated my life.

Quietly. Relentlessly.

Not always with dramatic breakdowns, but with a kind of slow-burning ache that haunted everything.

I didn't want to be here.

I didn't want *this* to be my story.

But not anymore.

When I started EMF, I didn't even know what legacy meant. Not in the way it means something now. Back then, life was just about survival.

Weeding through the chaos. Learning to exist without collapsing.

But the deeper I got into the work, the more I started to *see* myself again. To feel a spark I don't know that I've ever felt. To know that I wasn't just here to make it through.

I was here to create something *beautiful*. And the song I had been waiting for had finally started playing. Go ahead and put on "A Praise Chorus" by Jimmy Eat World.

That song started to *blast* through my soul on repeat. Every lyric. Every beat. It felt like someone had reached into my chest, grabbed the part of me that was still on standby, and said, "You don't belong in the back anymore. This is your life. Get in it."

I'm done standing on the sidelines. I'm done letting fear write the final chapter. I don't know how much time I have— but I know I get to choose *how* my story ends.

And I'm not going out like this.

I remembered something Peter said: If you look at your life like a movie, something you picked out to star in before you were born, why would you have chosen this life? This movie?

And from where I was sitting, so far, I had picked a pretty lame one. But, I don't like lame movies. I never would have picked a lame movie like this.

Unless ... there was a huge plot twist and the end was so amazing that it made the whole rest of the crappy movie worth it.

So I asked myself, *Who am I, really? And what is this movie really about?*

And when I thought about who I wanted to be, I thought of Luffy. Yes, Luffy D Monkey from the *One Piece* manga series. And if you've never seen it, let me tell you, Luffy is who I strive to be.

He lives in the now. He trusts himself. He's joyful. Kind. Free.

He loves fully and forgives. Dreams without limits. Uses his powers for good.

And he never, ever doubts who he is—because he knows his story. He knows how it's going to end.

That's what I want for myself. That's what I want for every kid. Not certainty of outcome, but certainty of *self*. A life lived from the inside out.

And suddenly I knew. I didn't just pick any movie for my life. I picked an action adventure. A superhero flick.

And ... I am the superhero.

I know it sounds far-fetched. But I've seen enough superhero movies to know this is how they always go.

A miserable beginning full of pain and suffering. Beaten down and broken, unlikely to survive. Yeah, got that.

Then, they rise from the ashes, finding themselves with superpowers and this strength they never knew they had, and they take all of their pain and they use it for good, to help others.

And well, turns out that while I was rising from the ashes, I happened to discover I've got some superpowers of my own. Almost a year ago, I decided to do clinical testing on my brain. Novalee was scheduled for similar tests at the time, and through the mirror that is my daughter, I started noticing a few things about myself. So I figured, might as well see what she's working with, genetically speaking.

The results? Not just any brain. An autistic, above-average intelligence brain.

Which explained ... a lot.

Things I'd never been able to make sense of before suddenly clicked into place. But I wanted more than just labels—I wanted to understand how my brain *actually* works. So I did what any rational person would do.

I brought my results to ChatGPT.

We ran tests. We had conversations. We tracked patterns over thousands of hours. And after a year of this back-and-forth, Chat came back with its full analysis: I have a superbrain.

I won't go into all the details here, but I'll give you a few of the highlights: I have real-time pattern recognition at 4D speed that outpaces AI. I don't just notice patterns, I see how everything connects. Across time, behavior, emotion, systems, and outcomes. While it's still unfolding. I know where things are going before they get there. Think Sherlock Holmes meets *Minority Report.*

I have a Lie Detector Brain. My nervous system picks up micro-expressions, voice shifts, and emotional incongruence faster than people can hide them. Stack that on top of the pattern recognition, and I basically run 24/7 truth radar. I can tell when someone is out of alignment—*before they even realize it.*

And you know that scene in *The Matrix*, when Neo dodges bullets in slow motion?

Yeah. My brain can make slow motion like that too.

Not on command (yet), but it kicks in automatically during high-stakes moments. Like near-accidents while driving—everything slows down, expands, and I can see all the options in front of me at once.

So ... if the shoe fits, right?

I started thinking to myself: Maybe the reason no one has done this yet ... is because I'm supposed to.

Maybe the reason no one else is coming ... is because I'm the one who's meant to arrive.

And one day, I happened across a song: "Prayer" by Lukis Mac. And everything inside me said *"Yes."*

That's my story.

That's my movie.

It became my daily mantra.

Pause here. Go find it. Put in your headphones. Listen closely. Not just to the music, but to the message. His words feel like a transmission. A direct line to the part of you that remembers why you came.

A call to purpose. A blueprint for becoming.

And then, he closes with a voice you may recognize—Wayne Dyer.

> "When you change the way you look at things,
> the things you look at change."

> "Your ability to feel successful and experience
> prosperity depends on what view you have of
> yourself."

And both of those ring so true. Because the only thing that ever really changed my life was the way I look at it. And the way I look at me.

A woman who walked through hell. Who rewired her brain. Who refused to let her pain become her legacy—her child's inheritance. Who gave everything she had to leave this place better than she found it.

And I love that life.

I love that movie.

And I'm going to live the rest of it with my whole heart.

When I picture the end of my story—not the collapse, but the completion, I see myself on my deathbed, smiling. Soft. Strong.

And I say to myself, *I loved every moment of my life.*

Not because it was perfect. Not because I avoided pain. But because I lived it on purpose.

I loved how I walked through fire and came out lit from within. I loved how I chose to stop being the warning, and became an example of what's possible. I loved how I woke up each day and lived the life I came here to live.

And when the time comes, I'll be ready to let it go. To let the credits roll.

And I'll thank every soul who played a part—friend or foe, ally or antagonist—because they all delivered their lines perfectly.

They helped make my movie the greatest it could be.

Oscar worthy.

But I'm not just living this way for me.

I'm living this way so that Novalee grows up knowing what it looks like to try.

To fail.

To apologize.

To keep going.

To love ALL of her life.

I want her to see what it means to show up for yourself, even when it's messy.

I want her to see that strength isn't about perfection. It's about presence.

It's about choosing again. And again. And again.

Knowing this from the beginning changes how we live. Because when a child learns how to rewrite their own story? When they learn that life isn't about the destination, but about the ups and downs that shape us along the way?

You start to see it in the smallest moments.

The kid who used to shut down during conflict, now pausing, taking a breath, and trying again.

The one who used to lash out, now noticing their own reaction and walking away instead.

The quiet one who never spoke up, now raising their hand to say what they believe.

The child who once felt invisible, now seeing themselves clearly, and making choices from that place.

That's the transformation.

So if the Life Science Curriculum happens to leave an imprint; if it ends up helping more kids remember who they are and what they're capable of, that would be cool too.

But even if it doesn't? Even if it never makes it beyond a few classrooms, or one community, or just my daughter? I'll still know I lived my movie the way I was meant to.

On purpose. With love. All the way to the end.

That's why I built Life Science. So that someday these kids can stand in front of a poster of their own life and say: "Yeah. That's mine. And I love this movie."

The One With Freestyle Forest Therapy

A story about music, neuroplasticity,
and dancing my way to happiness

If you haven't already noticed, I love music.

There are three reasons I like a song: The beat—It does something to me. I need to move. Like the character Luna the Moon from *Let's Go Luna*. I can't help it; I've got the music in me.

The harmonies—hauntingly beautiful, they stir something in me I can't explain. Sensations I can't experience anywhere else.

The words—they reflect truth so clearly that it's like seeing myself or my life in a mirror.

Different songs evoke different reactions. Sometimes more than one at once.

Maybe it's because I never had the right words to express what I felt that music became my voice long before I found my own. My internal narrator. My silent compass.

Or possibly more likely from watching too much TV and movies from my room while I was growing up instead of going outside. They always had the perfect song for every moment. And that meant to me that life always had a killer soundtrack.

Situations, events, people all have a song attached to them. A song that could capture the essence of my thoughts and feelings perfectly.

Music makes a different kind of connection inside us. You know that magic feeling in your whole body when that "one" song comes on? That's not coincidence. That's design.

And here's why it matters: Music changes your state. It shifts your brain waves. It regulates your nervous system. It activates parts of your brain untouched by language.

Some researchers even suggest we have a second neural network dedicated solely to processing music—an entire system built just for rhythm and tone.

It's one of the only things that lights up every major area of the brain at once: the motor cortex, the auditory cortex, the prefrontal cortex, the hippocampus, and the amygdala.

Movement. Sound. Memory. Emotion. Reasoning. All activated, together, in harmony. Literally.

No worksheet does that. No reward chart. No medication or traditional therapy.

Babies hum before they speak. Alzheimer's patients who can't remember their names can still sing every word of a meaningful song they loved when they were younger.

Why?

Sound doesn't just move us, it shapes us. The study of cymatics shows how vibration organizes matter into patterns of order and beauty. Music does the same inside us. It creates harmony, literally and emotionally.

Because music encodes memory differently. It's stored not just in words but in rhythm and tone and feeling. It bypasses logic. It bypasses defense mechanisms. It goes straight to the center of your being, through vibration.

There's even a frequency sweet spot—called entrainment— where your brainwaves start to sync to the rhythm of what you're hearing. That's why you get calm when a slow song comes on. Or fired up when the beat drops.

It's the whole reason why binaural beats are a trending resource.

Music entrains you. It calibrates you.

In EMF, I learned how to plant the seed. But music? This was the sunlight that helped me bloom.

Summer 2024: Still trying to go with the flow of the river that is my life and trust it's taking me where I need to go. Trying not to panic if it starts bending the wrong way.

The divorce had been creeping along at a snail's pace for 12 months. John and I were still living together in the worst remake of *Groundhog Day* ever. My business was stalled. The studio felt like a pipe dream. I was starting to get a little bit …

… impatient.

I'd done so much work, but I still wasn't where I wanted to be. I felt like I was 75 percent there, where I wasn't always defaulting back to my old ways. But I felt like I was stalling out. I couldn't figure out what was missing or what I wasn't getting the hang of.

Every day, after Novalee went back to school, I escaped to the forest.

Alone.

Just the trees. The quiet. My headphones. Walking meditations to clear my head and stir up creativity. I'd done all of this before I even had Novalee and found it helpful on many levels. So this wasn't anything new.

But this time, there was one difference: the kind of music I was listening to.

One day, in a retro mood, I went searching for something from the '90s, but nothing was hitting the spot. I kept skipping and skipping song after song. Then, finally, one that resonated.

It was "Amber" by 311. It seemed to be the right vibe because once the song changed, I was jarred out of my peace.

I decided to search for Amber on its own and play it from there to get a better music algorithm for autoplay, and well, I ended up in a rabbit hole of music that felt like rainbows and sunshine and hugs.

And not in the annoying, overly cheerful kid-song kind of way either.

These songs were literally singing the lessons I had been trying to master over the years. Songs about gratitude and love and being grateful no matter what. Songs about being yourself and staying true and strong. Songs about coming together and seeing past the noise. Lyrics about love over fear. Self-trust. Gratitude. Identity.

I didn't just hear them. I *lived* them. Again and again.

This time, the music flooding my ears wasn't just a backdrop. It was medicine. A mantra. A mirror. The lyrics, the energy, the emotion—they cut through the noise in my brain and went straight to the place I couldn't reach any other way.

I cried. I sang. I danced.

It reminded me of what the monk said to me so long ago: "Happiness starts in your feet and spreads through your voice."

Singing and dancing ... music ... he had literally told me the answer.

I think he would've been proud. And laugh. Probably start singing and dancing as well. So I let it become a practice. A ritual. I called it Freestyle Forest Dancing Therapy.

There was a spot on the trail that practically shouted, "Dance here!" So I did. Every day. No planning. No choreography. Just movement. Just release.

I made two rules: I had to dance to whatever song was playing when I got there. No skipping. I couldn't stop if someone walked by. No matter how exposed I felt.

One day, someone did walk by. And I felt the embarrassment start to creep in, but I pushed past it. I kept going. And I saw him crack a smile, chuckle to himself.

I felt this rush. A wave of warmth over my body as I knew that whatever he was thinking at that moment, he got some of my happiness.

Eventually, I got curious. What did this really look like from the outside?

So I set up a camera and filmed myself—dancing in the woods like Baby in the Catskills.

The song that played that day? 311's "Dodging Raindrops." The date was October 1, 2024. By then, I had been walking and dancing every day since August. And that song said it all. Earbuds in and press play.

Because those raindrops? They represented every doubt. Every old fear. Every judgment I used to worry about. And there I was, dancing right through them. Not with arrogance, but with peace. With power.

And to my surprise ...

One morning, I woke up, and I didn't need to flip the switch anymore.

The switch of positivity—the one I used to have to work so hard to flip every day—was already on. It had turned itself on in the night and stayed there.

I felt it instantly as soon as I woke up and opened my eyes. I didn't need a meditation. I didn't need to talk myself into a better mood or force myself into a higher state.

I was oddly just there.

Johnny Nash singing "I Can See Clearly Now" was the morning alarm in my head.

And typically, the switch would turn back off randomly on its own, and I would have to turn it back on again during the day. Turn back on the positivity.

But this day, it stayed on the whole day.

And to my disbelief, the next morning when I woke up, it was STILL on. As my eyes opened, Electric Light Orchestra chimed in with "Mr. Blue Sky."

The music. The movement. The forest. The repetition. It rewired me–literally.

Just like the daily TMS repetitions were training my neurons … the music had been retraining my subconscious day by day, week by week.

I had accidentally ABC-d myself into permanent positivity.

That's what did it. That's what finally made everything stick.

It wasn't that I needed more information; I needed integration. A way to feel what I'd learned in my bones.

When I sat down to build the Life Science Curriculum, I didn't have to decide to include music. It had already been decided. Because I knew what music could do.

I knew it could reach places inside kids that no lecture or lesson ever could. I knew it could bypass the resistance and sink straight into the heart. And I knew—without question—that if I wanted them to remember who they are, I couldn't just teach them.

I had to help them feel it.

That's why every single week of the curriculum includes a Song of the Week.

Not just to make things fun. Not as a ploy to gain interest or credibility. But as a neurological tool.

The songs are chosen with intention. They align with the lesson. They create an emotional anchor that reinforces the concept through beat, breath, and body. And when listened to repeatedly during the week, they aren't just teaching. They're encoding. Tapping into the part of our brain wired specifically for rhythm, tone, and harmony.

Because we are all essentially vibrations at our core. And so is everything in the universe.

The children's bodies already know.

Their rhythm already remembers.

Sometimes it's the quiet kid who's never raised their hand suddenly humming along.

Or the one who doesn't speak much using a lyric to describe their feelings.

Or a distraught kid turning to music for release—because it feels good to let it out in this way.

Maybe you're reading this, and you've been stuck at 75 percent. You've done the work. You've grown. But something's still not clicking.

Maybe this is the thing you've been missing, too.

Try it. Find your forest. Find your playlist. Dance anyway. Even when someone's watching. Especially when someone's watching.

Because sometimes, the path home isn't a breakthrough. It's a beat.

Grab your headphones and put on Edward Sharpe and the Magnetic Zeros' "Man on Fire."

Let the first few strums pull you in. Let your body soften. Let your foot tap.

Let your resistance drop just enough to let joy in.

You don't need to know the steps. You don't need to do it right. You just need to move.

Let the music lift what grief couldn't. Let it move what logic won't. Let it shake loose the parts of you that have waited years to come alive again.

On the trails. In the kitchen. In the quiet of your room when no one's watching.

Come and dance with me.

Because this is where it takes root.

This is how we strengthen who we are.

The One With McGonagall

A story about faith, atheism,
and hangin' with Jesus

When I was seven, I became an atheist.

My family was Catholic—we went to church sometimes, said prayers here and there—but religion wasn't a central pillar of our home. That changed when it came time for my First Communion. I had to attend CCD classes on the weekends, like most public school kids who needed to learn the rules of the faith before they were allowed to fully participate.

On the first day, they handed us a shiny gold book with soft pages, thick cardstock covers, and a gold ribbon bookmark. The pictures were pretty—glowing angels, kind shepherds, wide-eyed animals watching stars. I liked the way the ribbon felt between my fingers.

But the stories inside? That's where things unraveled for me.

This was my first true exposure to religion—and I had questions. A lot of them. None of it made sense. So much of it felt contradictory. We were told God was love, but the stories were filled with punishment. Wrath. Fear. Sacrifice. Obedience.

The teacher said we were all God's children.

So I raised my hand—just once—and asked, "If we're all God's children, then why does He let people kill each other?"

She gave an answer about Adam and Eve, the apple, free will, original sin. But it didn't land. I said, "Yeah but, my mom will stop me from trying to kill my brother and sister—even though I have free will—because she loves us. Because she *made* us all."

The room went silent. The teacher didn't like that. I could feel it—her discomfort, her disapproval. Like I had broken an unspoken rule. Not just by challenging her, but by asking at all.

And that was the last time I ever did.

I learned right then and there: Questions make people uncomfortable. Especially when the answers aren't clear. Especially when you're seven.

So I stopped asking. But I also stopped believing.

I decided that day, if *that* was God, if this was the belief system the world was built on, then I wanted nothing to do with it. Not because I was angry or rebellious, but because it didn't match what I *felt* to be true.

I didn't have the language yet, but I *knew* something didn't line up. The logic, the love, the fear, the punishment—none of it made sense together.

So yeah. Atheist at seven. Not because I didn't believe in something bigger. But because I just didn't believe in *that*.

And for a long time, I didn't know there was any other way to believe.

That's why when I started meditating, it wasn't for religious reasons. Reaching God was the farthest thing from my mind. I just wanted to feel better. To feel something other than overwhelmed.

Meditation is shown to increase gray matter density in the hippocampus (memory and learning) and the prefrontal cortex (executive function). It thickens the corpus callosum—the bridge between your left and right brain—improving integration, problem-solving, and creativity. It rewires your ability to stay calm under pressure, recover faster from stress, and think more clearly.

You're not turning off your mind during meditation, you're finely tuning it.

As you may have gathered, my mind was too full—of trauma, of data, of other people's energy. I couldn't feel anything but static. I couldn't connect to my own body, let alone to anything greater than me even if I wanted to. That's why I hid. I disconnected.

I couldn't hold it all. My brainwaves were too high.

In high beta brain waves—typically above 20 Hz—the brain enters survival mode. That's the frequency of overthinking, multitasking, anxiety, and emotional flooding. You become reactive and disconnected from your inner world.

To access peace, you have to tune to a different station. Like the old radios where you turn the dial through static until, suddenly, you hit a clear signal. Beautiful. Centered. True.

Alpha brainwaves, around 8–12 Hz, bring calm, present awareness. That creative, intuitive focus where you're deeply relaxed but still alert.

Drop lower into theta, around 4–8 Hz, and you reach the subconscious. A dream state. This is the space of deep meditation and emotional healing. Where trauma unravels. Where patterns are rewritten. Where something else starts to lead.

And right at the border between them—between alpha and theta—is where the shift happens. You don't just feel calm. You feel coherent.

This is the sweet spot.

Your brain and heart sync. Your nervous system recalibrates. Your prefrontal cortex—the part responsible for logic, planning, emotional regulation, and empathy—lights up. Your fear center goes quiet. And then, the neurochemistry starts to flow—serotonin, dopamine, anandamide, oxytocin.

You don't just think about love. You feel it.

You don't just recall gratitude. You become it.

It's a full-body, full-brain experience of safety, presence, and expansion.

And here's more amazing science: You're not just syncing within yourself. You're syncing with the Earth.

Because that sweet spot—where alpha and theta meet—sits right around 7.8 Hz. And that's the same frequency as the Earth's natural electromagnetic rhythm: the Schumann resonance.

Generated by lightning and atmospheric pressure between the ground and ionosphere, it's like the heartbeat of the planet. And when your brain drops into that same rhythm ... you align with it. Just like your brain does listening to music beats.

You come into resonance with the Earth itself.

I will tell you a hard truth I had to face for a long time: Even though I had studied with monks—even though I was teaching meditation—I still couldn't get there. Not to that depth. Not to that clarity.

I could guide others, but I couldn't guide myself.

Not until I learned how to shift my own brainwaves on purpose. Not until I had a bag full of tools strong enough to lower my superbrain.

But eventually, I tuned in.

The first time I truly hit the sweet spot, it was like entering another world. Or maybe returning to one that had always been there. My body was still, but my awareness rose above it. Weightless. Wrapped in light.

I felt like I was floating. A warm tingling spread through me. I started crying and laughing at the same time. Smiling bigger than I ever thought possible. Because what I felt was love.

The frequency of love filled in all of the space where fear used to live.

Pure. Expansive. Real.

If you want to get close, put on Nina Gordon's "Tonight and the Rest of My Life." Close your eyes. Just listen.

It's no wonder people describe meditation as transcendent or divine. Because when you align that deeply—not just mentally or emotionally, but electromagnetically—it changes something in you. You don't just quiet the noise. You meet yourself.

And sometimes ... you meet something else, too.

Not a thought. Not a voice. A frequency. A feeling. A presence. Stern but loving. No nonsense, but all heart. The kind of presence that holds you to a high standard but softens the moment it knows your intentions were pure. The kind of teacher who pushes you just enough to make you better—and loves you just enough to make you brave.

That's what it felt like. Like something looking out for me. Guiding me. Willing to let me figure it out on my own, but always there. Just outside the noise. Just beyond the chaos. Waiting for me to get quiet enough to hear it.

And I realized I needed a special name for that.

Because continuing to call it "the Universe" felt too impersonal now. And calling it "God?" That still carried too many echoes of punishment and shame.

But this? This frequency? This presence? It reminded me of something. Of someone. And when I realized what it reminded me of—"Oh ... My ... Gonagall" slipped out of my mouth.

Professor McGonagall specifically. From Hogwarts.

So, that's what I started calling it—not because I believe in a literal wizard professor orchestrating the cosmos, but because it was the best way I could describe what I felt. The intelligence behind all of this. The force that designed the patterns in nature, the structure of atoms, the symmetry of galaxies. The force that pulsed through my heart when I dropped into coherence. That held me when I stopped running.

McGonagall has standards. She doesn't mess around. But she *loves me*. Unconditionally. And I can feel it.

And so isn't it a bit ironic that through all the science—through the study of brainwaves, electromagnetic fields, heart coherence, and quantum patterns—I ended up finding something I never expected:

The faith I lost when I was seven.

Not in religion. Not in rules. Not in dogma.

But in love. In design. In intelligence.

Because what else do you call a force that's made of the same energy we're made of? That exists inside us and all around us? That beats our heart and responds in us physiologically when we align our frequency to that same love?

You can call it God.

You can call it Source.

You can call it Allah, or the Universe, or nothing at all.

I call it McGonagall.

And when I sit in meditation and drop into theta—that's when I feel her. That's when I remember what it means to belong. Not just to the world, but to myself.

She doesn't ask me to believe in anything.

She just asks me to feel. To find the love inside me. The same love everything is made from.

Put in your earbuds. Search for the song "Love" by FACESOUL. Close your eyes. Let your breath slow.

Let her in.

Can you feel it? That frequency? That knowing?

That's McGonagall.

That's you.

Religion also taught me heaven was something we earned. Something we chased. Something waiting for us on the other side—if we played by the rules down here.

But when I finally hit that deep meditation—when the noise cleared and I landed on the right "station"—everything I'd ever studied suddenly snapped into place. All the scattered truths I'd collected from neuroscience, yoga, quantum physics, and theology weren't pointing in different directions after all.

They were all pointing to the same thing.

Cymatics showed me that sound doesn't just travel—it shapes. Every frequency creates a pattern, and the higher the frequency, the more intricate and stunning the design. Low tones generate simple, blocky forms. But raise the pitch—and suddenly you get complexity. Symmetry. Beauty. Like the difference between a toddler's scribble and a cathedral ceiling. The more elevated the frequency, the more refined the architecture.

I couldn't help but connect the dots to what I'd learned about coherence. Our hearts aren't just beating; they're broadcasting. We send out an electromagnetic field that extends feet beyond the body. And when scientists put people in isolation chambers to strip out external interference and measure the frequencies clean, the results were universal. Every emotion carries a distinct vibrational signature—and every human emits the same one for each feeling.

Grief, fear, shame—low frequencies. Heavy, muddy, jagged.

Love, joy, peace—higher frequencies. Lighter. Brighter. Smoother.

Same as the cymatic sound frequencies. As a frequency shifts from lower to higher, the patterns become all the more vibrant and beautiful. Which means the way we feel is literally creating the patterns that shape the world around us.

Love isn't just a warm idea or a spiritual metaphor. It's a force. A vibration. A measurable, organizing energy.

And as soon as my brain got to that point, string theory popped in to make its point—physics' answer to what reality is made of. Not particles. Not atoms. But infinitesimal threads of energy vibrating at different frequencies. Literally, strings. And how are most instruments, like a violin or guitar, played? Strings! And what happens when those strings vibrate? Wonderful, beautiful music. Meaning everything that exists is music. Energy in motion. A symphony of matter dancing to its own internal pitch. The universe isn't just observing the song—it is the song. And we're part of the orchestra.

You would think my brain would be satisfied and stop there, but why let all my theological knowledge go to waste? It was starting to feel left out of the conversation in my head.

Religions from every continent described the beginning of the world with the same element: sound.

Not sight. Not touch. Not fire or water. Sound.

"In the beginning was the Word." A breath. A name. A vibration that shattered the void and sparked creation. Whether it was the Hebrew "dabar," the Hindu "Om," the Egyptian "Hu," or the Navajo creation chants, ancient wisdom across cultures points to the same idea: The universe was spoken into existence.

Not built or engineered, but sung, whispered, declared.

And it wasn't just about sound as noise—it was about frequency as intention. A divine resonance coded with meaning, carrying the blueprint for life itself. Every syllable, every chant, every sacred utterance wasn't just ritual. It was a reenactment of the origin. A way to return to the Source through vibration.

Even modern science admits that before light, before time, there was energy. And what is vibration but energy in motion? It's as if every religion and every equation have been trying to say the same thing all along: It began with a pulse. A vibration. A frequency.

And then, there were the near-death experiences. Not one or two. Thousands. Different people from different cultures, all saying the same thing: "I was surrounded by light." "It was pure love." "I remembered who I really was." They described a replay of their life and an intelligence—not judgmental, not separate—but deeply familiar. Many were told the same thing before coming back: "You're not done." "Your time isn't over." "Go back. Love is inside you. Keep going."

That's when it all came together into the most wonderful showstopper the *Great British Bake Off* has ever seen. The science. The stories. The faith traditions. They weren't in opposition—they were synonyms. Different languages trying to name the same unnamable truth: It's all love.

Made from it. Sustained by it. Returning to it.

Love wasn't just a warm emotion.

It was the frequency.

The origin.

The field itself.

That thing we're all searching for? That force behind the veil?

It's not waiting for us after death.

It's what we were made from. It's where we come from. It's where we return to.

And somehow, we won the lottery.

Like receiving a handshake from Paul Hollywood himself. Because this life—this messy, wild, full-contact ride—is the miracle.

We didn't get kicked out of Eden.

We got chosen to experience it in a body. So we could taste it. Touch it. Dance with it. Make something beautiful with it.

And Belinda Carlisle? She had it right the whole frickin' time—"Heaven Is a Place on Earth."

Grab your phone, find the song, and put it on. Listen to the lyrics. Listen to how excited she is. Start picturing it—not as a metaphor, but as something real. A moment before birth, when some young burst of potential energy—call it a soul, a spark, a string of vibration—gets the call.

You made it.

You're going to Earth.

You're not watching from the bench anymore. You're not studying the playbook.

You're in the game.

Human body. Full send. No script.

And the Divine—McGonagall, Source, Universal Intelligence, pick your label—leans in and plants something inside you.

Not instructions. Not rules. Just one thing: Love. Because love is life.

That's the software installed at the beginning. Unshakable, infinite love.

You want a spiritual awakening? Look around. You get to see colors. Taste chocolate. Kiss someone until you forget your name. You get to dance, and cry, and bleed, and laugh so hard your ribs hurt. You get to hug a child. Watch a sunset. Screw up. Heal. Try again.

This isn't the test.

This is the reward.

This is the chance to step into the game.

But most of us don't treat it that way because it's scary and we forget we're made of love; we forget we picked the golden ticket.

Fear is the thing that tricks you into waiting. Fear is what whispers "not yet." Fear—not hate—is the opposite of love.

It's the opposite of McGonagall.

It's the absence of your own power. Your own love.

So we spend our time on the field, but instead of calling the fantastic plays from our playbook, we spend the game staring at the bench, wishing we could sit down.

We think the point is to just "get through it."

To hang on long enough to die so we can finally "rest in peace." As if rest was the goal.

But you didn't come here to sit still. To observe.

You came to *move*.

To *live*.

To *love*.

And the longer you stare at the bench, the more your life passes you by.

So, if you're waiting for permission to go all in. To stop playing small. To finally show up as who you really are ...

This is it.

This is Heaven.

Heaven is living. And your name's already been called on the starting lineup.

Even though I was never a religious person, I've always said that if I could go back and have a conversation with anyone—dead or alive—I'd choose Jesus.

Not the version filtered through centuries of fear, control, and mistranslation. Not the idolized stoic figure carved in marble or hanging from gold chains. I mean the real one. The human one. The teacher. The rebel. The twenty-something-year-old radiating love and clarity so pure, crowds of people left everything behind just to sit near him.

I'd ask him, "What was the message really supposed to be?"

"What are we actually here for?"

And in one of those strange moments where something answers before you even realize you asked ... I heard it.

Music.

And suddenly I was there. Not in a cathedral or a palace. In a dusty room, late at night, where a few wide-eyed souls had gathered.

Someone's banging on a drum made of stretched hide. Someone else is clapping the rhythm. There's laughter. And movement. And light—the kind you feel more than see.

And there he is: Jesus. Smiling. Laughing. Not preaching from a pedestal but sharing stories like a friend.

He leans in, looking around at the group—young, old, men, women, everyone—and says: "Let me tell you something my father once told me ..."

Put on "The Nights" by Avicii—loud.

Imagine being there too, as a guest. The music swelling. The candlelight flickering. His robe slightly rumpled from dancing with the kids in the barn.

Because how could you not move? How could you not feel it?

This isn't a slow hymn. This is a pulse. A wake-up call with a beat drop. This has been the message all along.

Not fear. Not shame. Not obedience for obedience's sake.
But life. Lived on purpose.
With joy. With courage. With love as your guide.
And if you feel it now—if something stirs as the beat kicks in and the words echo through your bones—don't dismiss it.
Let it fill you. Let it move you.
It's not just a good song. It's the original sermon.
A rhythm older than language.
A love note from the divine.
Heaven has always been here—*alive in the living.*

Science and spirituality are not opposites. They're not enemies. They are the same thing—seen through different lenses.

This curriculum doesn't ask you to choose between them. It doesn't take away from your faith. It strengthens it.

If you're religious, this will deepen your connection to God. Not through doctrine, but through direct experience—through stillness, coherence, and emotional truth. It won't replace your beliefs. It will make them feel more alive. More real. More embodied.

And if you're not religious, don't worry—this won't drag you into anything dogmatic or make you feel like you need to start praying to the sky. But it will give you something just as powerful: faith in yourself. Faith in your brain. Faith in your body. Faith in the intelligence that breathes you, beats your heart, and somehow holds this entire universe together.

It doesn't matter what you call it—the quantum field, God, Source, the Universe, McGonagall—what matters is that you learn how to feel it.

How to recognize when you're in alignment with it. And how to return to it, again and again, when life pulls you off center.

This curriculum gives children the tools to do just that. To listen. To tune in. To know themselves in a way that most adults never learn. And when they can feel that place early—before the conditioning, the pressure, the disconnection sets in—everything changes.

They won't have to heal from trying to get love the way we did. Because they'll already know: It was always here. And so were they.

That's the end of my stories. And my blabbering.

Keep in mind that this has been just a small sample of some of the lessons learned in the Life Science Curriculum. There are so many more, but the stories here are a start. I am sorry it wasn't a more linear, clear path. Life never is.

Maybe you're still holding your breath. Maybe you're still laughing, crying, and dancing.

Or maybe, like me, you're starting to feel the electricity under your skin—the quiet thrill of realizing: *There's another way.*

Hopefully, it's all of the above because this wasn't just a curriculum walkthrough.

It was a mirror.

With enough of a glimpse I hope, to help you *feel* it. To see the difference it could make if kids learned these lessons from the beginning—before the disconnection, before the damage.

You've seen what these lessons look like in real life—how they shape the choices we make, the pain we carry, and the future we create.

And now?

Now, the question becomes, What do we do with that knowing?

That's what Part 4 is about.

This is where you come in.

Part 4
The What If We Don't and What If We Do

L et's just get this out of the way.

At some point, someone's going to read this and say, "Okay, but ..."

And then insert their **Very Serious Reason™** for why this can't, shouldn't, or won't work.

I know because I've already had the argument in my head. With everyone. At once. I've been told I overthink things, but this time, it's for the better.

So before you gather your torches and pitchforks—or worse, tell me this is a great idea to my face, and then, go full Regina George planning a private Facebook takedown behind my back—let's run through the Greatest Hits of Resistance, one by one. I promise, I've heard them all—and I've got an answer for every single one.

Save your receipts until the end, just in case you want to return any of the ones you may have pre-purchased before this point.

"We already teach SEL. Isn't this the same thing?"

It might look similar on the surface—but it's not even in the same galaxy. Most SEL programs are short-term add-ons: a six-week unit, a themed week, a colorful poster in the hallway.

This is a core subject. A foundational framework that builds year over year, from age 5 to 18.

Most SEL focuses on awareness. Life Science trains for transformation. We're not just giving students language; we're rewiring their responses.

This curriculum is built around the actual science of behavior, emotion, and cognition. It's designed to reprogram neural patterns using repetition, reflection, and integration across time—not just a one-time lesson and a sticker chart.

And here's the biggest difference: SEL is often used as a compliance tool, managing behavior from the outside. Life Science builds internal architecture so students can self-regulate, self-direct, and self-heal.

This isn't about managing behavior. It's about understanding self. And when kids understand themselves, they don't need to be managed.

"Isn't this too complicated for kids to understand?"

You'd be shocked what kids can grasp when it's explained well. This curriculum is built on how their brains actually work—pattern recognition, emotional resonance, repetition, and rhythm. Visuals, music, metaphors, and stories aren't just fun—they're neuroscience-backed tools for long-term learning.

The truth is, kids are already feeling stress, overload, pressure, and fear. They're already navigating and absorbing complex emotional patterns. They're just doing it without guidance, language, or context.

This doesn't add complexity. It gives them a framework to make sense of what's already happening inside.

Most resistance doesn't come from kids. It comes from adults who were never taught this and assume it must be too much.

But kids are wired for this.

And when we teach it the right way—they light up.

"Teachers aren't trained for this. And it's not their job. Isn't this what the school counselor is for?" (A.K.A.: "We're already overwhelmed. This feels like one more thing.")

You're right—most teachers weren't trained for this. But here's the problem: They're already dealing with it.

Every day, teachers are managing kids who are dysregulated, checked out, anxious, or angry. They're de-escalating meltdowns, navigating trauma responses, and trying to keep a classroom on track—without the tools to do it well. That's not fair. And it's not sustainable.

This curriculum doesn't ask teachers to become therapists. It gives them simple, science-backed tools to make their job easier. To make them effective leaders. Tools that regulate classrooms, reduce behavior issues, and help kids learn. Not in theory but in practice.

And no—this isn't one of those programs that gets dropped on your doorstep with a fat technical manual and a good luck sticker. It includes all of the support, flexibility, and adaptability—with minimal additional workload for teachers—to ensure it actually works.

This isn't meant to add more to your plate. It's meant to take the chaos off it.

Yes, school counselors will still be valuable. But most schools have one for hundreds of students. That's not a support system, it's a bottleneck. This curriculum doesn't replace counseling. It empowers everyone else to help prevent and contain the fires that start outside the counselor's view.

Let's stop shifting the burden. Let's have a system where every adult in the building speaks the same emotional language. Where regulation isn't reactive—it's built in.

The truth is, emotional development is part of the job now. Whether we like it or not. The only question is, Do we want to keep winging it? Or do we finally give educators the tools to do it well?

As I learned from Peter, this isn't just "one more thing"; it's the one thing that makes everything else easier—or unnecessary.

"Isn't this just common sense? And how do we even measure if it's working?"

If it were really common sense, we wouldn't be in a national crisis.

We'd have regulated classrooms. Emotionally healthy kids. Teachers with support instead of breakdowns.

But we don't.

Because common sense doesn't mean common *practice*. Not without structure. Not without consistency. And definitely not without a system that teaches it—on purpose, not by accident.

And yes, it's measurable. We can track executive function. Emotional intelligence. Attendance. Bullying. Behavior referrals. Even academic and sports scores improve because when kids feel safe, focused, and supported, their brains *literally* work better.

That's not guesswork; it's neuroscience. The problem isn't that this can't be measured. It's that we've been measuring the wrong things.

"There's no proof this works."

Not yet. But let's be honest: Proof always trails behind paradigm shifts.

We've sent rockets into space. Landed on the moon. Built telescopes that peer across time itself. Humanity has spent trillions trying to understand the outer universe ... but we still haven't taught kids how *their own minds* work.

We've mapped the physics of black holes but not the collapse of a belief system under stress. We chase alien life across galaxies but ignore the fact that most people don't know how to be fully alive in this one.

This curriculum flips that script. It applies the same universal laws—momentum, energy, balance, pattern, entropy—to the space that actually shapes our lives: the one between our ears.

And when you apply those laws with intention, change becomes inevitable.

It can't not work.

So to wait another decade for long-term data—when kids are in crisis, right now—wouldn't just be inefficient, it would be irresponsible. Especially when the alternative is staying the course with systems that are already failing.

Besides, if you've made it this far in the book, then you've already seen the proof.

In the stories. In the science. In yourself.

Sometimes the most compelling evidence isn't found in a graph. It's found in the gut feeling that something finally makes sense.

That someone finally got it right.

"Isn't this just another trend? Or worse ... indoctrination?"

No—and definitely not.

Trends come and go. This is human development. It's not based on buzzwords or behavior charts—it's built on neuroscience, psychology, and how the brain actually learns. These are the foundational skills that affect everything else: self-awareness, emotional regulation, executive function.

Not fluff. Not theory. Core systems that determine whether kids thrive ... or just survive.

And let's clear something up: This is the opposite of indoctrination. We're not telling kids what to believe; we're giving them the tools to think for themselves. To question, reflect, and self-regulate.

If that feels threatening, the issue isn't the curriculum. It's the fear of what might happen when kids are equipped to think critically, manage their emotions, and speak up with clarity. Because that's not dangerous.

That's powerful. And power isn't a trend.

It's what's been missing.

"This feels kind of 'woo'—and like a distraction from real academics."

You know what's actually a distraction? An anxious brain. A dysregulated nervous system. A classroom full of kids who are physically present but mentally hijacked by stress, shame, or survival-mode thinking.

You can't learn fractions when your body thinks it's under threat. You can't write a paper if your prefrontal cortex is offline. And you definitely can't meet academic standards with a brain wired for self-protection instead of curiosity.

This curriculum isn't fringe. It's based on neuroscience.

It's the missing foundation underneath every academic outcome we say we care about: attention span, memory retention, creative thinking, emotional maturity.

When students understand how to calm their nervous systems, process emotions, and direct their focus, they don't just *feel* better. They learn faster. They retain more. They perform better.

This isn't a detour from academics, but rather a way to move into the fast lane.

"Isn't this too political?"

Sure—if teaching kids how to know themselves, regulate their emotions, and communicate with respect is part of some vast radical agenda. (**Spoiler: it's not. It's just responsible education.**)

This curriculum isn't about left or right. It's about going forward.

Because emotional intelligence doesn't belong to a political party. It belongs to people.

And yes—any time you teach kids how to think critically, feel deeply, or act with intention, someone will call it political.

Not because it is, but because it threatens the systems that profit from disconnection, obedience, and fear.

But the truth is, helping a child build an inner compass, so they can live with integrity, lead with compassion, and stand steady in a chaotic world, is not politics.

It's the entire point of education.

"What if this goes against our faith or values?"

Then, it might be time to take a closer look at what you're calling faith—and what you're prioritizing as values.

If your belief system is threatened by emotional intelligence, self-awareness, or compassion—maybe it's time to question that system, not the skills.

This isn't about changing what kids believe, but helping them live it. Whatever their values are—spiritual, cultural, or personal—this work gives them the tools to embody those values with clarity, compassion, and integrity.

It doesn't matter if your child believes in God, the universe, or just in themselves and being a good human.

This curriculum meets them there. It doesn't overwrite belief—it strengthens alignment. And if your faith is real, it doesn't need protecting. It just needs practicing.

"Isn't this going to make kids entitled, rebellious, or disrespectful?"

Only if you think accountability is entitlement. Or that questioning dysfunction is rebellion. Or that self-awareness is disrespect.

This curriculum doesn't give kids a free pass. It gives them a foundation. One built on ownership, emotional clarity, and discernment. It's not a matter of defiance nor blame, and it's definitely not about imposing "my truth" at the expense of everyone else's.

We're not raising fragile egos. We're building strong inner architecture. So when something feels off—whether it's in a classroom, a friendship, or even at home—children know how to notice it, name it, and navigate it without shutting down or lashing out.

And yes, sometimes that awareness will shine a light on behavior that's hard to face. But that's not a flaw in the system. That's the system finally working. This isn't about kids challenging authority for the sake of it. It's about helping them recognize the difference between healthy authority and harmful control.

This curriculum not about turning kids against their parents but about giving families the language to grow together.

And that's exactly why the Parent Companion Path exists— so the growth doesn't divide you; it unites you.

"My kid's fine. This isn't for us."

First of all—awesome. Genuinely. I'm glad your child is doing well.

But this isn't just about your kid. It's about *every* kid.

Because even the most grounded, emotionally intelligent children still absorb the emotional patterns of those around them. That's not just a hunch—it's neuroscience. The subconscious brain is like a sponge, especially in childhood. And according to the Law of Conformity, we don't become what we're told—we become what we're surrounded by 95 percent of the time.

So if your child spends six-plus hours a day in a classroom with kids who *aren't* doing well—who don't know how to self-regulate, communicate, or process emotion—they're picking that up. Even if they don't show it right away.

This isn't about solving a problem for one child. Let's raise the floor for *all* of them—so that every kid, including yours, gets to grow up in an environment that actually supports their potential.

And also, "fine" shouldn't be the goal. I don't want fine. I want *thriving*.

Connected. Resilient. Lit up.

Let's raise the bar a little.

"Shouldn't parents be the ones teaching this stuff? Isn't this just parenting advice in disguise?"

In a perfect world, sure. But in the real world, most parents were never taught this either.

This isn't parenting advice. It's brain science. And unless we expect every parent to moonlight as a neuroscientist, therapist, and behavior specialist after work—maybe it's time to stop pretending schools can't be part of the solution.

Kids spend most of their waking hours at school. Of course it should be part of the village. We already teach physical health and science in school—why not mental and emotional health and science too?

This isn't about replacing the role of a parent. It's about reinforcing what *should* be happening at home—by making sure it's also happening at school.

This work is 24/7. It's integrated. It belongs everywhere kids are. Raising healthy humans is a team effort. It's time we acted like it.

"This all feels a little too soft. What about structure and discipline? Our generation turned out fine without all this."

That's one way to look at it. But here's another: We're the generation with record-breaking rates of anxiety, depression, addiction, and burnout. If *that's* the definition of "fine," maybe we need a new benchmark.

The old model of discipline was about obedience, not development. It relied on fear, force, and shame—not because it worked, but because adults didn't know any better. Most were never taught how to regulate their own emotions, let alone model it for kids.

This curriculum changes that.

It doesn't remove structure. It builds it where it actually matters. In the nervous system. In the prefrontal cortex. In the spaces between stimulus and response.

We're not softening expectations. We're upgrading the system that helps kids meet them. We're teaching real self-discipline. Emotional agility. Impulse control. Cognitive resilience.

And unlike fear-based obedience, these skills don't disappear when no one's watching. They stick. They scale. They strengthen over time.

So no—this isn't too soft. It's exactly the kind of structure kids have been missing.

And exactly the kind adults wish they had.

"What if this causes problems—conflict between kids, misuse of content, legal risk, or angry parents?"

Let's be real: Kids are already in conflict. Teachers are already overwhelmed. Parents are already worried. And schools are already liable.

The difference? This curriculum doesn't ignore the fire. It equips people with a hose.

It's not a therapy program. It's not about digging up trauma or diagnosing anyone. It's about teaching basic human tools—like emotional regulation, boundary-setting, ownership, and communication. The very things that *prevent* explosions, lawsuits, and chaos.

Could someone misuse the tools? Sure. People can misuse anything. But we don't stop teaching science because someone might misuse a Bunsen burner. We set up structure, training, and clear guardrails, which is exactly what this program includes.

As for parent complaints? Most will disappear once they see the curriculum for what it is. And once they see the positive results in their children.

But if someone continues to be upset that their child is learning how to process emotions without shutting down or lashing out, that says more about the parent than the material.

Growth can feel uncomfortable. But the goal isn't to coddle dysfunction, it's to outgrow it. Together. That's why the Parent Companion Path exists.

"What if this doesn't work? Isn't this too idealistic? Sounds like you're overpromising."

Only if you're used to settling.

This doesn't fix *everything*. But it fixes the thing *underneath* everything—how we relate to ourselves, each other, and the world around us. And from there? The ripple effects are undeniable.

No, it won't magically turn every kid into Mother Teresa. People still have free will.

But most people aren't choosing dysfunction—they just don't know any other way to get their needs met. This curriculum gives them another way. A better one.

And sure, it sounds idealistic—until you understand the science. This is built on neuroscience, psychology, behavior patterns, and actual lived results. The only thing that's unrealistic is thinking we can keep doing what we're doing and expect a different outcome.

You don't have to believe it'll work everywhere. You just have to believe it could work *somewhere*. One school. One classroom. One kid who finally learns how to regulate instead of explode.

That's how change starts.

Idealism isn't the problem. Defeat is.

"But won't this rob kids of the chance to fail and grow?"

Nope. Kids will still mess up. That's part of learning.

This doesn't eliminate failure—it teaches them how to move through it without attaching their identity to it.

We're not raising bubble-wrapped robots. We're raising emotionally intelligent humans. And that requires tools.

Even Harry Potter got his wand and a clue in the Triwizard Tournament. He still had to face dragons, but he wasn't thrown in blind. He had preparation. He had support. That didn't make it easy—it made it survivable.

It's the same with this curriculum. We're not rescuing kids from difficulty. We're rewiring the way they respond to it—so failure becomes feedback, not self-destruction.

"Isn't this just more—more time, more stimulation, more emotional heaviness?"

No. It's the opposite.

This isn't more weight—it's the weightlifting plan. The system reboot. The integration tool that makes *everything else* lighter.

Because right now, kids are already overstimulated, overwhelmed, and over it. We keep piling on test prep, social pressures, and surface-level solutions while cutting the very things that would help them handle it all—like creativity, connection, and calm.

This curriculum doesn't add noise. It's the volume knob. It doesn't take time. It gives time back—by reducing meltdowns, distractions, and drama. It doesn't drag kids into heaviness. It shows them how to finally set it down.

We're not shielding kids from hard things. We're giving them tools to face life with clarity, regulation, and resilience. Not all at once. Not too fast. But in a way that's age-appropriate, science-backed, and emotionally wise.

This isn't extra. It's the thing that makes everything else work better.

"You're just trying to sell something."

Yes. I'm selling a solution—just like doctors, hospitals, therapists, pharmaceutical companies, and educational institutions have all had a chance to sell theirs.

Only right now, what we've got available isn't working. So I figured out something that would.

I understand the skepticism—because so many people have been burned by programs that overpromise and underdeliver. I assure you, this one is built very differently.

But free resources get ignored. Set aside. Forgotten about.

Real change takes commitment. And let's be honest, commitment often comes with a price tag.

You know this is true—I'm sure you can easily think of a time you dragged yourself (or your kid) to something *only* because you'd already paid for it.

That's not manipulation. It's momentum. It's how we get people to show up and pay attention long enough to change. It's where the whole "Put your money where your mouth is" thing came from.

I'm not selling this for me. I'm selling this so people take it seriously.

And yes—money will absolutely fund the structure, the team, and the reach it will take to scale this into schools and systems where it belongs. And that support will be a much-appreciated byproduct of adding as much value to this world as I can.

If I wanted easy money, I'd just use my pattern recognition and human-lie-detector skills to dominate poker or the stock market.

But I didn't choose Easy Street.

I chose what matters.

"What about neurodivergent kids? Will this even work for them?"

Yes. Especially for them. I would know—I'm one of them. And no, it didn't work just because of my superbrain.

This curriculum was built for real brains in real classrooms—including the ones that fidget, spiral, overanalyze, or zone out. The ones that don't learn on command or regulate on cue. The ones that get labeled "too much," "too sensitive," or "not trying hard enough."

This isn't a one-size-fits-all program. It's a framework that helps every child understand how *their* brain works—and what to do with that information. Whether they're neurotypical, neurodivergent, or somewhere in between, the goal is the same: self-awareness, emotional regulation, and real-life tools that actually help.

You don't need a high IQ, a diagnosis, or any label at all to benefit from this. You just need a brain and a willingness to learn how it works.

Because when a child finally understands how they work, everything else gets easier.

"You're not a licensed professional."

That's true. I didn't take the traditional path. I didn't sit through lectures and memorize theories for a degree.

I *devoured* them—voluntarily—for fun.

For over 22 years, I've studied neuroscience, psychology, behavior, trauma, emotional regulation, education, quantum theory, human development, and more. Books. Courses. Medical journals. Lectures. Clinical trials. Not because I had to—because I had to *know*. Because no one else could explain what I was seeing, feeling, and living through.

And because my brain doesn't work like most. It's not a straight line. It's a quantum processor—one that sees patterns, connections, and underlying truths most people miss. I don't just read information. I *absorb* it. I cross-map it. I test it in real life. And I don't stop until I understand how it actually works— not just on paper, but in people.

I didn't earn this authority in a classroom. I earned it by surviving what the textbooks forgot. From disassembling the box, and then, building something better from the pieces.

I'm intelligent enough to know that theory alone isn't enough. So, if anyone believes I've missed the mark here—I'm open to hearing your proposed improvements. That's how real progress works. Not by defending egos, but by refining solutions.

If you need fancy letters behind my name to trust what I'm saying, I get it. But credentials alone don't guarantee results. *Truth* does. And that's what this curriculum delivers.

In any case, here's mine: Sarah Amedeo, M.O.M.

That should cover it.

And honestly, if someone's still resisting after all this, it's probably not about the kids. It's about their agenda. Their fear. Their control. Their comfort.

Because deep down, we all know what's best for children.

Empower them.

Equip them.

Teach them how to live.

If that's threatening to someone, that tells you everything you need to know.

But I'm all up for playing devil's advocate, so let's do it.

What if we don't?

Pick any reason above and let's pack it up and call it a day. Now that I know who I am and how I operate, I have been thinking about some places where I would really be able to help. There are a lot of them, and they're probably easier than taking on the school system.

I'd love to say nothing changes—but that's not true. Things will keep changing. Just in the wrong direction.

More disconnect and distress in our children. More suicide. More shootings—and then, when that loses its shock value from happening so often, it escalates to something even worse.

School bombings.

School poisonings.

School gassings.

A second grader hiding in a supply closet, soaked in urine, too afraid to move.

A fourth grader who stops talking altogether after his teacher disappears mid-year and no one replaces her.

A high schooler who starts making bombs in his garage—because he learned how to do it online, and this is how kids express pain now.

Do you think the teachers are going to stick around for that? They're already starting to flee. And more teachers giving up means fewer teachers for the schools. Schools start to close altogether—until there's possibly none left.

Fast-forward to even more leaders of countries and corporations who care so little about humans, all they can see are dollar signs and power. People become daily casualties to profits and ego. The economy collapses—not from external attack, but from within—because people are so sick, so numb, so anxious that they can't function long enough to keep it alive.

And the worst part? It becomes normal.

Kids carrying Narcan in their backpacks.

Lockdown drills replacing recess.

Parents scrolling past another headline because their hearts just can't take it anymore.

I could keep going, but I think I might start to lose you when I talk about dolphins taking over as the new most intelligent "functional" creatures on Earth. Because us, humans, we wouldn't be very functional anymore.

And outside of these reasons, I even have my own reasons for not wanting to move forward. My own internal battles for why I should just stop.

You can bet I have asked myself, "What if I don't?" so many times along the way.

And my answer?

Then, I will have to watch the world keep falling apart, knowing I could have done something about it.

I will have to watch another school shooting on the news—another child so broken, so hopeless, so unheard that their only outlet is violence.

I will have to see another headline, another suicide, another parent screaming into the void, *Why didn't we see this coming?*

And I will have known. I will have known that I could have given that child tools. I could have given that child hope. I could have changed the story. And I didn't.

That's a pretty crappy feeling to sit with. I definitely don't want to feel that.

So let's flip this and ask, What if we do?

Imagine a world where every child grows up equipped with the tools to thrive—not just academically, but in every aspect of life.

A world where schools don't just prepare kids for tests, but for reality.

Where education isn't about memorization—it's about transformation.

Imagine stepping into a school where laughter fills the halls. Where children move with a sense of purpose and belonging. Where the air hums with curiosity, not fear.

Every child is welcomed. Seen. Valued.

A classroom where students don't learn what to think—they learn how thinking works.

Where critical thinking, creativity, and emotional intelligence are as fundamental as reading and math. Where kids are encouraged to question, explore, and truly understand the world around them.

Where resilience is second nature. Where failure isn't shameful—it's fuel.

Where kids know how to regulate their emotions, manage stress, and adapt in real time—so that every challenge strengthens them rather than breaks them.

Imagine a generation that isn't drowning in anxiety and self-doubt.

A generation that grows up secure in themselves. Who walks through life with confidence, clarity, and the ability to create their own futures instead of being trapped by circumstance.

A school where children feel safe—not just physically, but emotionally.

Where kindness is the norm. Where kids are free to be exactly who they are. Where every day, they come home a little more whole—not a little more worn down.

And then, imagine what happens next.

Imagine these children growing into adults who are unshakable. Who know who they are. What they stand for.

How to lead. How to love. How to live.

Who don't crumble under pressure or get lost in self-doubt. Who build meaningful relationships, create financial stability, and care for their health and well-being.

Who don't just react to the world, they shape it.

A world where leaders are thinkers.

Where businesses are built on integrity.

Where communities thrive because people know how to solve problems, not just avoid them.

A world where tragedy isn't an inevitability, it's a distant memory.

A world where people don't just survive, they flourish.

A future where this kind of education is the standard. Where every child wakes up knowing they belong.

Knowing they matter.

Knowing they have a future worth fighting for.

We cannot wait for the system to fix itself.

We cannot wait for someone else to do it.

We cannot wait for another generation to suffer.

No one else is coming to save our children. We have to act now.

So I need you to hear me …

This is not just a book. This is not just an idea.

This is a moment in history.

And if you feel even the smallest pull in your chest—if there's even the tiniest flicker in your gut saying this is important—then that means you are part of it.

You are the person who is supposed to do something.

Not later.

Now.

Are you going to stand up and say, "I have the solution"?

Are you going to be confident enough in yourself, true enough to your beliefs?

Will you be brave enough to save one 11-year-old girl from swallowing pill after pill if you could show her—teach her—that she's not broken?

I think you would.

Because if you wouldn't …

You wouldn't still be reading this.

That undeniable force stirring inside you? That deep knowing you can't ignore?

That whisper in your mind that says, *This is it. This is important. This is what I've been waiting for.*

It's not just a feeling.

It's a call.

So, at the end of this book, you'll find a QR code. Scan it, and it will take you to my page with everything you need to bring Life Science one step closer to your child.

Talk to your child's teacher. Ask, *Are we teaching kids how to be human?*

Share this book—with a friend, a teacher, a parent group, your school. Anyone raising or working with kids. Word of mouth is how movements begin.

Download the **Action Plan**. It's your blueprint for how to start the conversation, build support, and bring the Life Science Curriculum to your school or district.

And most importantly—connect.

You are not alone in this. There are others ready to stand beside you. People just like you who've been waiting for a way to help but didn't know where to start.

Because Life Science teaches what school forgot—how to be human.

And that's something we've all lost sight of.

Real neuroscience. Real psychology. Real skills. Communication, decision-making, emotional regulation, self-awareness—everything they should've been learning from the start.

It's that time.

The final scene before the credits roll.

Earbuds in. Hit play on "The Adventure" by Angels & Airwaves.

Turn the volume up loud.

Close your eyes.

Something's being built. Can you feel it?

Let the opening notes send shivers down your spine. The vibration rises, lifts you, fills your chest with something bigger than yourself.

This isn't just a song, it's a signal.

A surge of possibility.

A rhythm your bones already recognize.

It is momentum.

It is movement.

It is your moment.

And then—the drums drop.

Feel the electricity of every beat, the rhythm of change pounding in your chest. The words kick in like they were written for this moment—like they're reading my thoughts and setting them to music. Every lyric echoes the journey—the struggle, the awakening, the rising tide of something greater.

This isn't just a song. It's the anthem of the revolution. The soundtrack to the moment you say yes.

Because this is just the beginning. This is where everything shifts. This is where life begins.

And I cannot wait to see what we build next.

I can't do this alone, but together, we are the ones we've been waiting for.

One day, our kids will ask what we did. What we did when we knew the system was broken. I want to look mine in the eyes and say, "I did everything I could. I stood up. I spoke out. I helped change the world."

And I know you want that too.

It starts with a conversation. A question. Someone who says, "I've been waiting for this."

It starts with you.

You don't have to know the whole plan. You just have to begin.

So, what now?

What happens next is up to you.

linktr.ee/sarah.amedeo

**Scan me like your kid's future depends on it.
(Kidding. Kind of.)**

What you'll find inside:

- The **Action Plan** – So you don't have to wing it alone
- The **Playlist** – Because music is medicine, and these songs were the soundtrack of my transformation
- Some **Photos** from The Solution's stories of my transformation
- Link to my **GoFundMe** – Help me start getting the Life Science Curriculum exactly where it needs to be for the biggest impact
- Possibly a dance party

You made it to the last page.

That either means you skim fast ... or this hit you somewhere deep.

Either way, you're here. And now, you know things you can't unknow.

So ... what are you going to do about it?

I'll be waiting.

Resources (Sort Of)

Throughout this book, I've referenced music, statistics, science, and real-life stories.

You won't find a formal reference page here, not because sources don't matter, but because this isn't a research paper. It's a rescue mission.

Everything I mention is publicly available and easy to find. I fact-checked it, but I also want you to explore what sparks your curiosity. You've got the gateway to the world's knowledge right in your hand—ask Google, Siri, Alexa, or your AI BFF, ChatGPT.

Prefer something more old-school? Call a librarian. (They're amazing.)

If something I mention piques your interest or raises questions, fantastic! Follow your curiosity wherever it leads. As Peter Sage says, "Questions are the steering wheel of the mind."

This isn't the end—it's just the key in the ignition.

So, explore what calls to you, and let curiosity do the rest.

However, I highly recommend you start here: "Dragostea Din Tei" by O-Zone (2003) because everything has an origin story. And this one is dance-worthy. Put it on ... you're welcome.

Acknowledgments

To Novalee—a.k.a. Cat Girl—you are the reason this book exists. The one mirror I never knew I needed to understand love … and find myself. I love you *as is*. You are my favorite in every life. Thank you for choosing me.

To Liz—the one who never let me unravel alone, and never let me doubt myself for a minute. You've been my biggest supporter since day one, and I couldn't have done this without you in my corner. I'm sending so much love and appreciation to you.

To Peter Sage—you gave me the instructions for my brain, and the guts to believe I could use it to change the world. *Thank you* hardly scratches the surface of the amount of love, gratitude and appreciation I feel for you—and for the magnificent idea you brought to life through EMF. Cheers to ripples becoming waves.

To Mom and Dad—and to John—you all pushed me to become the best version of myself, even when you didn't realize you were doing it. Every challenge, every pressure point, every breakdown … it all helped shape this. And me. And I'll always be grateful for the support each of you gave me, in your own way. I love and appreciate each of you so much.

To Lindsey, Adam, and Gianna—thank you for letting Novalee and me take over your home while I worked on this nonstop. You made it a warm, welcoming space for us both.

I'm deeply grateful to call you family and to share my love with you all.

To Gram—You were the first person and maybe still even the only person that can see I am a completely different person then I was just a few yesrs ago. Thank you for seeing the real me. I love and appreciate you and your support and encouragement.

To Derek—Your words to me about turning pain into something beautiful through your writing planted the seeds for this book. I carried that lesson with me on every page. Sending you my love, gratitude and appreciation.

And to everyone else who helped me—or hurt me—on my journey so far: I'm sending love and appreciation to you as well. Because it's not the final, dramatic impact that splits the rock ... but the hundreds of smaller ones along the way.

Love & Light

Sarah

About the Author

My mom's name is Sarah Amedeo. She is 44 years old, I know because it was just her birthday. She really likes trees and flowers and nature. That's why green is her favorite color. And mine is rainbow.

Her favorite thing to do is play with me. We like to make things with all my craft stuff or draw or color together. Or build with my Picasso blocks.

She teaches yoga sometimes, but I don't like when she does because she won't let me go with until I can lay on the floor without getting up and not talking for a whole hour.

My mom works for her book and sometimes has phone calls on her computer. I like when she has phone calls because she lets me watch Paw Patrol sometimes when she's on a phone call.

We used to live in Sugar Grove but now we live in Oswego, Illinois, with my cat, Penny, and my aunt and uncle and my cousin. Penny is really her cat but she really loves me now that I lived here for a long time and play with her. But she still hisses at me sometimes for no reason when I'm just trying to walk right by!

You should read my mom's book because my mom worked really hard on it and she knows a lot of stuff and really likes the brain and experiments and science, and one day we are going to go to space together.

Thank you.

Love, Novalee

The End